Focus on Teaching

An Introduction to Education

FOCUS ON TEACHING

AN INTRODUCTION TO EDUCATION

SYLVESTER J. BALASSI

Paterson State College

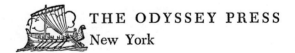 THE ODYSSEY PRESS
New York

To Eileen

Preface

Focus on Teaching: An Introduction to Education is designed to be used as a basic or supplementary text in preservice teacher education courses, especially the introductory course. Rather than attempting to survey all areas of the broad field of education, this book focuses on teaching while examining those areas of education believed to be of most interest and/or importance to the student. The author's experience with the introductory course over a period of years indicates that the student is primarily interested in material related to *teaching,* for often he is attempting to decide whether or not to pursue a teaching career. Some of the "how to" of teaching normally found in methods courses is therefore included as teaching is examined at all levels from preschool to the university. In addition to assisting students already enrolled in formal courses, this book may be helpful to others considering teaching as a career—high school or college students seeking a college major or adults interested in entering the teaching profession.

An effort has been made to introduce the student to the "new" in education and to the many changes now taking place in the schools. Such topics as the following are included: the major curriculum developments and reforms; the Head Start Program; the nongraded school; programed learning and teaching machines; team teaching; the middle school; the education of the socially and culturally deprived; the ever growing community college movement; the 1967 report of Dr. James B. Conant on the comprehensive high school; and the education of the gifted, the slow learner, and other fields of special education. At the same time, the student becomes acquainted with such educational leaders and innovators as Robert H. Anderson, B. Frank Brown, Jerome S. Bruner, James B. Conant, John I. Goodlad, and Jerold Zacharias.

Introducing the student to the literature of the field is an important aspect of a first course in education. For each chapter, therefore, a dozen or more selected references are provided with annotations to aid the student in further reading. Effort has been made to include the works of leading writers and up-to-date references for the particular area under study. Furthermore, ample footnotes are provided in most chapters as a guide to authoritative sources. Appendix A contains a list of fifty professional periodicals to illustrate the great variety of journals available and to direct the student to those in his special field of interest.

Study may begin at several points in the text. The author begins with a general consideration of teachers and teaching in Chapter 1. Others, however, may wish to start with Chapter 6, "The American Public School System," which provides an overview of the historical development of the American public school system and the way in which it is organized and financed at the national, state, and local levels. Actually, study could begin with Chapter 8, "Careers in Education," or even with Chapter 9, "Teaching All Children and Youth." The instructor is free to adapt this book to his particular course. He may expand on any chapter in the text or add other units of study as he sees fit. To aid the instructor further, a list of suggested activities for the class is provided at the end of each chapter and a list of films for use in the course is given in Appendix B.

The author wishes to express his deep appreciation to Dr. Eileen C. Balassi, his wife, for all her talented assistance and to

Professor Alice M. Meeker for the chapter she contributed on early childhood education. Thanks are also due to Miss Judy Le Protto who assisted in typing the manuscript.

S. J. B.

Contents

Focus on Teaching

An Introduction to Education

1 Teachers and Teaching

Commitment to teaching as a career, as a profession, and as a way of life is essential in order for one to be successful and happy as a teacher. This commitment is made easily by a few, with difficulty by many, and not at all by some of those who are preparing to teach. Actually, some people make this commitment to teaching only after several years of experience in the classroom. Whenever and however the commitment is made, it involves a great deal. Let us examine some of the factors involved in making a real commitment to teaching.

First of all, it seems to the author, there must be a liking for children or young people and a desire to help them to grow and learn. Working day after day with children is difficult indeed if one does not enjoy being with them. You may like children individually, but how do you feel about them in groups? You may feel that you want to work in kindergarten, but even a day spent in observing twenty-five frisky five-year-olds may change your mind.

It takes a keen interest in adolescents, for example, to carry a teacher through some trying times with these young people. Do not feel that you are going to be faced by a class of thirty high school students who will be interested in nothing but what you will attempt to teach them. Many of these boys and girls will be much more interested in each other than they will be in what you are going to teach. They will "try you out," and try your patience in the process; they will attempt to determine what kind of class control you will have. It will be up to you to provide this control for them.

Second, there must be a desire to learn and grow; for once you have committed yourself to teaching you have committed yourself to a life of learning. The statement of John Cotton Dana, "Let he who dares to teach never cease to learn,"[1] is surely an apt one. No one's education ends with graduation, least of all the teacher's. You must like learning, for you will have to do a great deal of it. You must be willing to give up some of the time you would ordinarily spend in leisure in order to keep up to date. Newspapers, general periodicals, professional journals, significant books, and new texts are only some of the things you will need to read. Workshops, conferences, conventions, and other professional activities will fill your calendar. The life of the teacher is a busy one indeed, and a good part of that life must be spent in learning and growing.

Third, there must be a willingness to give of one's self, to give knowledge and time and effort and care to others. This does not mean that you cannot have a life of your own, but it does mean that you cannot be completely self-centered. You must care enough about your students, your work, your school, the betterment of society, and the future. You must be able to give of yourself to these things. If you cannot give what is asked, then find something else to do with your life, something other than teaching.

Fourth, this commitment involves a willingness to accept certain restrictions which may be imposed on one's private life simply because he is a teacher. To be sure, the image of the teacher is changing, but his conduct is still subject to public scrutiny. In some areas of the country this scrutiny is more severe than in others, for what the public expects of its teachers varies. In a small conservative community, for example, the teacher may be expected to live on a higher moral plane than others; in a larger

---

[1] Motto inscribed on the library building at Newark State College, Union, N.J. Mr. Dana, of the library staff, devised the motto.

city, though the restrictions on a teacher's private life may be fewer, his conduct must still be above average.

Fifth, though teachers' salaries are improving, one must be able to accept the hard economic fact that as a teacher he may not be able to afford the standard of living offered by other professions. It is one thing to accept this in theory; it is another matter to live it. Not that the teacher will lead an impoverished life, for he will not. It is more that he will not be able to give his family some of the things he would like them to have.

As a younger person looking ahead to life, your decision to accept the teacher's standard of living may not be a realistic one. This is probably one reason why many young teachers leave the profession. You must think through carefully what it is you want in life, what really matters to you, and be certain that a teacher's salary will provide this for you.

Sixth, real commitment requires complete involvement with the students you are teaching. Complete involvement means that you accept fully the responsibility to know and to become interested in your students; that you actually do get to know them as individuals; and that you make use of this knowledge in your teaching. It is, of course, much easier to treat the class as a group and to teach them that way. To know them as individuals takes time and effort, but this time and effort will reap dividends: your teaching will be more effective and your experiences with students richer. A student must become more than a name on a seating chart to you. He must become the warm, live, and different individual he really is.

WHY TEACH?

There are probably many reasons, both conscious and unconscious, why people teach. Some of the reasons given frequently by students preparing to teach are considered below.

The influence of former teachers is surely a factor. As one student put it: "I admired the great way they had with children and how whenever you were around them your whole day seemed to brighten up." The desire to render social service, to help people, and the satisfaction this brings about, is frequently voiced. A prospective kindergarten-primary teacher wrote: "It [teaching] gives you a purpose on earth, answering the question everyone naturally asks of himself—'What am I doing here?'" Or, as another student phrased it: "After helping someone I have a feeling inside me that really I can't describe." Other students have said: "I want them [pupils] to get started on the right foot"; "I want to help the young grow to be fine adults and citizens"; "I want to help the future generations of our country get a proper education."

Perhaps the most common reason for wanting to teach given by preservice teachers of younger children is a liking for such children and a desire to be with them. Those who want to work with adolescents, on the other hand, often mention that they enjoy their particular subject or field: "History has always been my most interesting subject" and "I have always liked English" are two examples. Experience shows, however, that one needs to be interested in the youngsters he is to teach as well as the subject he is to teach.

Some have other reasons for teaching. "When I considered teaching, I was thinking about what I could do for myself as well as for others," said one speech arts major. A physical education student gave these reasons: "It is a field I can always depend upon. For a girl it pays good money, the hours aren't that bad and I have the summers off. After I'm married I can always fall back on it in case I need to." "The hours of this job are very feasible for a woman who might be running a household as well as a job," was the view of a young lady in speech correction. Obviously, not all people are attracted to teaching as a career because of their love for children or young people.

Of course, there are some students who are really not certain of their decision to teach as they begin their study. "I'm still undecided. I'm hoping my first semester will clarify in my own mind whether or not I really want to teach," is a typical comment. It is hoped that this volume will be of particular help to such students.

Why do *you* want to teach?

WHAT ARE THE CHARACTERISTICS OF AN EFFECTIVE TEACHER?

Not everyone would agree on what the characteristics of an effective teacher are. Though research has been done,[2] this research has not yet given us a definite answer to the question.[3] As one experiences and observes teaching, however, one is struck by certain characteristics of teachers which seem to make them effective. The author would like to discuss some of the characteristics he has observed in working with students, student teachers, beginning teachers, and experienced teachers over a period of years. Hopefully, the attempt on his part to set forth these characteristics will evoke some speculation and discussion on your part.

Characteristics of an Effective Teacher

The discussion of the characteristics of an effective teacher which follows is not meant to be all-inclusive; it is simply a compilation of characteristics which the author believes to be among the most important. Your class, without doubt, will be able to add others.

Commitment. It is the view of the author that one must be committed to teaching in order to be effective in all aspects of the work of the teacher. This is why it is listed first among the characteristics. Since we have considered this question of commitment in the preceding pages, we will not repeat the discussion here.

[2] See, for example, David G. Ryans, *Characteristics of Teachers: Their Description, Comparison and Appraisal* (Washington, D.C.: American Council on Education, 1961), or A. S. Barr and others, "The Measurement and Prediction of Teaching Effectiveness: A Summary of Investigations," *Journal of Experimental Education*, 16:203–83 (June, 1948), or W. W. Charters and Douglas Waples, *The Commonwealth Teacher Training Study* (Chicago: University of Chicago Press, 1929).
[3] American Association of Colleges for Teacher Education, *College Teachers Look at College Teaching*, AACTE Study Series Number 8 (Washington, D.C.: the Association, 1965), p. 87.

Suffice it to say that most teachers who are truly effective teachers are committed to their work.

Intelligence. While it does not always follow that the higher the intelligence the better the teacher, the effective teacher does have above-average intelligence. This may not necessarily have evidenced itself in college grades, for often the "C" student does a fine job in student teaching while, on occasion, the "A" student does rather poorly. It well may be that the "C" student in such a situation is the more creative person and that his creativity has resulted in a superior teaching performance.

The effective teacher also needs to have sound judgment and good common sense, for he must make many decisions in the course of his work. These decisions involve such things as the length of time to be spent on a particular unit of study; the method of evaluating achievement; the reasons why a student behaves as he does; and the method of motivating the class for tomorrow's lesson. Often there will not be a great deal of time to think over what you will do or how you will respond to a specific situation. Therefore, you need to be alert and able to make decisions quickly.

Foresight is another important facet of intelligence. You have to anticipate a good many things in teaching. Many discipline problems, for example, are really teaching problems which could be avoided if they were anticipated. An integral part of lesson planning, to illustrate further, is having the foresight to know how students will react to a certain presentation and what kinds of questions they may ask.

Knowledge. The effective teacher has at least five kinds of knowledge: general knowledge, knowledge of what he is to teach, professional knowledge, knowledge of the students he is to teach, and knowledge of himself.

Let us hope that in this day and age we can all agree that if anyone needs to be well educated it is the teacher. Let us further hope that the days of insufficient general education for the teacher are gone forever. It is not the purpose of this volume to set forth particular percentages of various kinds of education for the teacher. Stress, however, is placed upon the need for a good general education.

The effective teacher must have a thorough knowledge of what he is going to teach. Yes, the teacher does teach *young people,* but he must teach them *something* and he had better know that something very well. This means that not only does he need a good foundation, but he needs to continue to learn, as was pointed out in our discussion of commitment to teaching. Knowledge is expanding so rapidly that it becomes more and more difficult to keep abreast of new knowledge.

Having knowledge is one thing; getting it across to students is another. The effective teacher must have a good knowledge of how to teach. Methods courses properly conceived and taught can contribute significantly to the developing teaching skill of the beginner. Since good teaching involves the use of a variety of methods, it takes the beginner some time to develop skill in the use of all these methods.

Included under knowledge of how to teach is also the ability to manage the physical environment of the classroom. Such factors as temperature, seating arrangements, distribution of materials, and orderly functioning of the class all have their effect on learning.

Professional knowledge certainly is not limited to teaching methods; there are many other branches to such knowledge. For example, professional education includes knowledge of why we teach (philosophy of education), knowledge of how we came to teach as we do (history of education), knowledge of how to evaluate (educational measurement), and so on.

The effective teacher must have a good knowledge of the students he is to teach. He must come to understand the behavior of the particular age level with which he is to work. Courses in human development and behavior are most helpful, but the teacher-to-be must also obtain experience in actually working with children or young people. Reading and studying about the behavior of children is one thing; being responsible for a group of lively boys and girls is quite another matter.

Finally, self-knowledge is most important to the teacher. He must know his strengths and weaknesses, his own capabilities for teaching. He needs to develop a thoughtful conception of his worth and overcome barriers within himself. Unfortunately, many programs for preparing teachers do not foster the development of such self-knowledge. Yet, according to Arthur Jersild, the chief difficulties teachers have, particularly beginning teachers, ". . . lie not in the outer and academic dimensions but in the inner and personal dimensions of the teacher's life."[4]

Sound character. Much could be written about the character of the effective teacher. The purpose here, however, is to focus attention on certain central aspects of the teacher's character: those aspects which have to do with the teacher's relationships with children and young people.

Fairness and freedom from prejudice are qualities one hopes to find in a teacher. Unfortunately, however, it is not always easy to be fair, nor to be free of prejudice. Not all boys and girls will appeal equally well to you. There are bound to be some whom you like better than others, and some you do not care for at all. Likewise, there will be students who do not like you, no matter how hard you try. You must accept this and not let it affect your professional relationship with them. *Professional* is the key word. For if you are to be professional you must treat all students equally. You must not let what prejudices you have show. Care must be exercised, for prejudice can operate at an unconscious level. Be certain, for example, that your respect for the dignity and worth of the individual is actually carried out in your day-to-day dealings with children.

Integrity is a vital quality. Students will expect that you will keep your promises, so do not make promises (or threats, for that matter) that you cannot keep. Students will also look to you to act on principle and to be consistent. What was proper behavior for a student in your class yesterday should not become improper behavior because of the way you *feel* today.

[4] Arthur T. Jersild, "Behold the Beginner," National Education Association, *The Real World of the Beginning Teacher* (Washington, D.C.: the Association, 1966), p. 44.

Be honest with your students. If you make mistakes admit them. If you do not know the answer, say that you do not know. Of course, you cannot say "I do not know" every day, for students will doubt your capacity. However, it is better, on those occasions when you do not know, to say so than to attempt to "bluff" your way through. A class will very quickly catch on to your bluffing.

You will carry a great responsibility in your classroom, for you will set standards for your students; you will be the arbiter of right and wrong, of good and bad. All of this you will do by some set of values, your values. It is imperative, therefore, that your ethics be of a high order. Teachers are not expected to be perfect, but they are expected to have sound values and a desire to help the young acquire sound values for themselves.

There are other character traits that could be discussed—dependability, responsibility, and sincerity, for example; however, discussion will be limited to those traits previously mentioned. The point is that the teacher should be a person of fine character who is aware of the responsibility he has in molding young lives and is willing to give the best he is capable of in carrying out this responsibility.

Good physical and mental health. While you do not have to be a perfect physical specimen in order to teach, you do have to enjoy reasonably good health. Teaching requires a good deal of energy and stamina. You will be surprised to find how tired you are after a day of teaching, particularly when you first begin to teach. You will soon realize that you will have to watch your health habits carefully in order to be effective in the classroom. Late-night television may be quite entertaining, but it may be something you will have to forego to function well the next day.

Good mental health is indeed important for teachers. The need to have your emotions under control, to have a generally cheerful outlook, and to have a healthy and wholesome view of others should be self-evident. The classroom is not the place to bring your problems—keep them outside where they belong.

Sometimes teachers tend to forget how much they contribute to the atmosphere of a classroom and to the attitudes of students. To a great extent you determine the amount of tension present, the cooperativeness and receptivity of students, and, in general, the climate of learning in that room. You owe it to your students to come in each day in as good a frame of mind as possible. At times this will be difficult but none the less necessary.

Enthusiasm. Enthusiasm can do wonders for your teaching. It is that something extra that arouses interest in the students and helps to get the material across to them. Some people are naturally enthusiastic; others are not. If you are not so blessed, you may have to work hard to develop enthusiasm in your teaching. It will be more than worth the effort, for it is the "magic" that can get a class stimulated even on the rainy Monday following a vacation.

Sense of humor. A good sense of humor is a real asset in teaching, an asset that can "save the day" in many situations. But let's be clear about what is meant by a good sense of humor: the ability to see the humorous side of things, to be able to laugh with the class, and, most of all, to be able to laugh at yourself. Do not attempt to be "funny" if you are not naturally so, nor should you inject humor at an inappropriate time. Properly used, your sense of humor can be a very effective teaching tool.

Flexibility. The need for flexibility is found in all phases of the teacher's work. You will have to keep a close watch on your flexibility, particularly as the years go on. It is all too easy to slip into a "rut" in your teaching; to become rigid in your planning; to stifle creativity; to ignore capitalizing on a sudden student interest; in short, to become inflexible.

Situations, circumstances, and events will make it necessary for you to be flexible:

the film you were to show does not arrive
a fire drill is called
the first snowfall of the season begins in the middle of your lesson
the chicks suddenly hatch in your incubator
the student who was to give the *pro* side of the debate is absent
a major news event occurs.

Any of these items will mean that you may have to deviate from your original plans. If you are flexible, you will adjust rather easily to the change required; if you are not flexible, the situation may be quite distressing.

The ability to take constructive criticism well and to act upon it is a part of being flexible. Many student teachers and beginning teachers do not seem able to do this. They become defensive and argumentative, neither of which helps them or the situation. Try to develop the attitude that the beginning years in teaching are learning years. You will not know everything about teaching when you are graduated from college. There are people who can and will help you. Accept their help.

Skill in human relations. The effective teacher must have the ability to work well with other people. Not only must he demonstrate good human-relations skills in the classroom, he must make use of these skills in dealings with other members of the staff, administrators, and parents. Whether the person involved be the custodian, the art specialist, the department head, or the principal, the teacher must enjoy good relations with him.

Pleasing appearance. Perhaps it seems unnecessary to say that the teacher should be neat in appearance and well groomed, but too often teachers seem to feel that their appearance does not matter. They forget that students have to be with them and look at them for some time each school day.

Make the most of yourself through appropriate and tasteful dress. You do not have to be a fashion plate, but do not become dated by the style of your clothing. The way we dress often affects the way we feel. Dress in a way that makes you feel poised and self-confident. Add a dash of dignity and a generous amount of refinement, and your appearance will be that of a professional person ready to do a professional job.

Effective voice and good speech habits. Not everyone is fortunate enough to have a voice that is rich and most pleasing to the ear, but such a voice is not essential for teaching. The teacher's voice, however, must be effective—effective in that it is clear and audible, has variation, and arrests attention. Your voice is probably your most important teaching tool; do all that you can to improve its quality.

Good speech habits are essential. Your speech should be clear, you should enunciate distinctly, and your pronunciation should be correct. There should be no defects or annoying mannerisms in your speech. Try to eliminate the repeated use of one word (such as *now*) or remark ("you know," for instance). Students have been known to spend much of their class time tallying the times the teacher repeats a particular word or remark.

Patience. One of the most important characteristics of the effective teacher is patience. It is a quality that comes into play in the teacher's work over and over again. It is best dispensed in large quantities daily, at very frequent intervals.

WHAT DOES THE TEACHER DO?

Subsequent chapters of this book will deal with the work of the teacher at all levels from the nursery school to the university. Before considering teaching at specific levels of education, an introductory overview of the teacher's work will be presented.

The Work of the Teacher

According to the Research Division of the National Education Association, the average work week for the secondary teacher is 48.3 hours and for the elementary teacher 46.5 hours.[5] The work week of some teachers is longer and the work week of others is shorter, for these figures represent averages. It is apparent that teachers do *work,* and many of them work quite hard. Let's examine some of the things that teachers do.

Teaching. Obviously the first job of the teacher is teaching. Teaching involves, among other things, planning, securing materials, presenting content, asking and answering questions, guiding

[5] NEA Research Division, *The American Public-School Teacher, 1965–66* (Washington, D.C.: the Association, 1967, Research Report 1967-R4), p. 27.

or leading discussions, giving assignments, checking work, and evaluating achievement. At the same time good discipline must be developed and maintained. Here is where many young teachers have their major problem. They do not want to be "strict" because they desire so much to be liked by the children. What they do not realize is that they are failing to provide the controls children want and need. Most of us would agree that the best control is self-control, but it takes time to develop this in young people. Do not expect to accomplish the task in a week or two.

In order to teach, the teacher must first plan. This takes time and much thought, particularly when you are a beginning teacher. In your initial teaching you will need good plans that are quite complete. Such plans will get you through some "tight spots." It is wise, at the start, to plan more than you can do in the time allotted. Then, you may not find yourself in the position of the new teacher who planned a forty-five minute lesson only to find that he was out of material and ideas in fifteen minutes!

In addition to planning, the teacher must prepare and/or secure materials of instruction. This may take the form of duplicating material, ordering a film or filmstrip, securing samples or illustrations, or selecting pictures or other visual materials. A word of caution about the use of audio-visual equipment—always be prepared for a breakdown! You never know when the projector will "give out" and you will find yourself with twenty-five minutes of time for which you had not planned.

Now that the planning has been done and the necessary materials secured, the actual teaching must be undertaken. It must be remembered that the teacher is "teaching" not only when he is addressing the whole class, but also when he is working with small groups or individuals. In an attempt to meet individual needs, much work is done today in small groups.

There is more to teaching than you may have thought. Teaching is not merely telling. In its best sense, teaching is stimulating and guiding learning. This may be done through a variety of methods, but an attempt to motivate students to learn must first be made. Students will learn well the things which they want to learn, the things in which they are interested. It is your job to try to get them interested so that they will want to learn. This is no easy task in the school "for all the children of all the people."

Method must suit purpose. If it is your purpose to "cover" much content in a short time, then a lecture presentation may seem appropriate. If, on the other hand, you wanted students to become involved in and with content, then a lecture presentation would not be appropriate. You perhaps would want them to participate in discussion after guided reading and experience that is as realistic as possible. At any rate, you would attempt to select a method that would accomplish your purpose. The proper selection of method is often the difference between effective and ineffective teaching.

Well-devised assignments correctly given are also a mark of an effective teacher. Too often assignments are not given sufficient thought by teachers, and they become no more than "busy work" for students. There ought to be a reason for an assignment and an objective it seeks to meet. Furthermore, assignments need not always be written. Visiting, viewing, and simply thinking, for example, can have much value.

Checking students' work can require large amounts of time. Just consider the situation of a high-school English teacher who has five classes of thirty students each. Assume that he assigns one theme a week for each student. Let's say that he spends ten minutes on each theme. Do you realize that it will take him more than twenty-four hours to go over these papers! This is in addition to any quizzes or other work he may have given. You may not have thought of the paper load in teaching, but it can be considerable.

Evaluating student achievement is probably one of the more difficult aspects of teaching you will experience. You may feel quite secure in saying that 85 percent is a "B." But what does that really mean? Does it mean that on a particular test given at the end of a marking period the student knew 85 percent of the material? If so, did that test represent all that the student should know about the material? Was the test an easy one? Then, 85 percent may not represent real achievement. Was the test difficult? Then, 85 percent may be an outstanding performance. But what does one test say about day-to-day interest and activity of a student? What does it say about his attitudes and behavior? Perhaps these few questions will give you some idea of the difficulty of evaluation. Courses in tests and measurements, though helpful, will not give you all the answers because the human element is involved. It is the human element that makes teaching a challenge, an ever new activity, and a satisfying career. It is the human element, the student, that teaching is all about.

Nonteaching duties. There are many nonteaching duties for the teacher. These include such things as keeping attendance records, making announcements, ordering supplies and equipment, keeping track of milk money and other small funds, completing reports, lunch duty, homeroom, study hall, club programs, meetings, committee assignments, and working with the P.T.A. Certain aspects of this side of teaching are less desirable to many teachers. They feel that some of these things, frequent announcements, for example, get in the way of teaching. The number of reports and memos to go over in some schools borders on the unbelievable. Other things, such as lunch duty and hall duty, could really be done by nonteaching personnel. Some schools are moving in this direction. But, to be realistic, teaching does have its share of undesirable chores to be done.

Guidance. Guidance is an integral part of teaching. There may be formal facilities for guidance in your school, but these will not eliminate the need for you to provide guidance for your students. The relationship that is built between student and teacher is such that guidance is a normal concomitant of that relationship. You know the student as an individual; you work with him daily. It is only natural that he should look to you for help and advice in many areas.

There are areas of guidance, however, that are beyond your competence and responsibility as a teacher. For instance, it is not within your province to provide psychological therapy for a student. You are not competent to do this, nor is it your function.

Your responsibility is identifying the possibility of such problems and referring the student to those qualified to help. This referral is usually made through your principal or the chairman of your department.

Reporting to parents. An important part of the work of the teacher is reporting to parents on the progress of their child. Though many schools use the traditional report card, some schools make use of the parent conference. Here the teacher gets together with the parent or parents to discuss the child's work at school. In such a situation the teacher's human-relations skills will be tested. It is not always easy for parents to be "objective" about their child. After you have discussed the child's strengths, you will have to be most tactful in discussing his weaknesses. Such conferences, nevertheless, can be a good way of reporting to parents, a source of helpful information about the child, and a means of promoting a better understanding between the school and the home.

Working with people. The teacher works with many people. Of course there are the students and the parents mentioned above. But there are many others: principals, department heads, supervisors, special teachers, fellow teachers, secretaries, and custodians. The teacher has relationships with these people almost daily; it is important for the effectiveness of both the school and the teacher that these relationships be good.

Sometimes it is difficult for the young teacher to win acceptance among his fellow teachers. Often he hinders his own cause by adopting a know-it-all attitude. He is quick to criticize what he sees as wrong in others and the school. It would be better if he were to take a humbler stance and attempt to be less critical.

If, as a new teacher, you do have suggestions of value, make these suggestions to the right people in the proper manner. Talk with the principal or your department head about a new procedure you wish to suggest. This is far better than spending your time in the faculty room complaining to others about the way things are done. Try to take care of the little annoyances and irritations of today, so that they do not grow into tomorrow's major problems. If, in time, there is too much in your work situation that really disturbs you, seek employment elsewhere. You will be happier and so will the school.

Part of working with people is maintaining good community relations. This surely requires that as a teacher you know your community and take an interest in it. One place where all teachers can work for improved community relations is right in their own classrooms. Every day twenty-five or more ambassadors, your students, go out into the community with an impression of the school and what it is trying to accomplish. You can do much to see that their impressions are favorable and that their reports of what goes on at school help in interpreting the work of the school to the community.

Professional activities. In addition to regular department and faculty meetings, there will be grade-level or subject-area meetings to attend. There will also be workshops and conferences. All of these will be added to your normal working day.

You will probably want to continue to study, either for further development or advanced degrees. Summers can be used for this purpose, though you may take course work during the school year, as do many teachers. Be careful, however, that you do not undertake to do too much, particularly in your first year of teaching.

Time must also be found for your professional reading. Though it will be hard to find the time, make the effort to keep up on your reading. It is an essential part of your continued growth as a teacher. You may find that you will have to put over to summer or holiday time reading which cannot be completed during the regular work week. Budget your time as is necessary, but be sure to allow sufficient time for reading.

You will probably want to join organizations to which your fellow teachers belong. There are such organizations at the national, state, and local level. The National Education Association and the American Federation of Teachers are the principal national groups for teachers; these two organizations, frequently referred to by their initials—the NEA and the AFT—are now competing

strongly for membership and for the right to represent teachers at
the local level. Some believe that the NEA, the far larger organization, is a "professional" group while the AFT, a union, is not.
AFT members, of course, do not share these views. They believe
that teachers have the right to organize within a union and to
seek collective bargaining with school boards. The union has used
the strike as a weapon, an illegal procedure in many states, but so
have some teacher groups affiliated with the NEA. In recent
years, both groups have become more militant.

The decision to join the NEA, the AFT, or neither group is
yours to make. Before making such a decision, however, you
would want to secure much information about both groups. In
Appendix C, you will find the Code of Ethics of the NEA,[6] which
can be used by you and your class as a beginning point in your
examination of these organizations.

This chapter has attempted to present the principal factors involved in a commitment to teaching, to review some of the reasons why people do teach, to examine some of the more important characteristics of the effective teacher, and to view significant aspects of the work of the teacher. The purpose has been
to introduce you to teaching, particularly some aspects of which
you may not have thought, and to stimulate you to rethink your
decision to teach. As you read the chapters which follow, you
will get a clearer picture of what it means to teach at the level
you have chosen. It is hoped that this reading may help you in
making a firm commitment to teaching.

SUGGESTED ACTIVITIES

1. Interview three teachers to determine why they chose teaching as a
   career and what satisfactions they have received from their work.
   Prepare a report of your findings.
2. Read and prepare a report on one of the many fictional or bio-
   graphical books on teachers or teaching, such as Bel Kaufman's *Up*

[6] The AFT does not have a code of ethics as such, but descriptive materials may be obtained from the nearest Federation office.

the Down Staircase or Jessie Stuart's *The Thread That Runs So True.*

3. With your instructor's approval, invite a superintendent to speak to the class about the qualities he looks for in employing teachers.
4. Select the most effective teacher you have had thus far in your education and prepare a theme in which you describe what it was that made this teacher so effective.
5. Rate yourself on each of the characteristics of effective teachers presented in this chapter. Do the results of this self-rating suggest that teaching really is the field for you? If so, in which areas of personality and character do you need further development or improvement?
6. Arrange with your instructor for the teacher-placement official in your college to speak to the class on the demand and supply for the kinds of teachers your institution prepares.
7. Plan to undertake some leadership experiences with children or young people to help you in deciding upon the level at which you should teach. Examples of possible experiences are scout leadership, camp counseling, and church work.
8. Compile a list of the best professional magazines available in the teaching field or level you have chosen.

SELECTED REFERENCES

Biddle, Bruce J., and Ellena, William J., eds. *Contemporary Research on Teacher Effectiveness.* New York: Holt, Rinehart and Winston, 1964. A useful guide to many research studies relating to teaching ability. Extensive bibliography.

Conant, James B. *The Education of American Teachers.* New York: McGraw-Hill Book Company, 1963. Recommendations for the improvement of teacher education based upon a study conducted by Dr. Conant.

Highet, Gilbert. *The Art of Teaching.* New York: Alfred A. Knopf, 1950. Considers teaching as an art, not a science, and presents examples of great teaching.

Kaufman, Bel. *Up the Down Staircase.* Englewood Cliffs, N.J.: Prentice Hall, 1965. A poignant noval about teaching in an urban secondary school.

Koerner, James D. *The Miseducation of American Teachers.* Boston:

Houghton Mifflin Company, 1963. Criticisms of teacher education and recommendations for improvement based upon the views of the Council for Basic Education.

National Education Association. *Teaching Career Fact Book*. Washington, D.C.: the Association, 1966. A helpful guide in considering teaching as a career. Contains information on teacher supply and demand, preparation and certification, salaries, conditions of work, and other related areas. Good list of sources for further information.

National Education Association. *Who's a Good Teacher?* Washington, D.C.: the Association, 1961. A summary of research concerned with measuring teaching effectiveness.

National Education Association, Research Division. *The American Public-School Teacher 1965–66*. Research Report 1967-R4. Washington, D.C.: the Association, 1967. A report on the personal and professional characteristics of teachers based upon a scientifically selected sample of classroom teachers.

Richey, Robert W. *Planning for Teaching*. Third edition. New York: McGraw-Hill Book Company, 1963. The first two parts of this book may be particularly helpful to the prospective teacher: Part One discusses aspects of planning for teaching, and Part Two considers teachers and their work.

Ryans, David G. *Characteristics of Teachers: Their Description, Comparison and Appraisal*. Washington, D.C.: American Council on Education. 1961. Presents the findings of extensive research on the characteristics of teachers.

Sharp, Louise D., ed. *Why Teach?* New York: Holt, Rinehart and Winston, 1957. Contains many statements of prominent people about teachers.

Stuart, Jesse. *The Thread That Runs So True*. New York: Charles Scribner's Sons, 1948. Traces the author's educational career which he began as a seventeen-year-old boy teaching in a small and lonely community.

Weber, Julia. *My Country School Diary*. New York: Harper & Row, Publishers, 1946. A detailed diary, kept by the author, of her four years of teaching in a one-teacher rural school.

2 Teaching the Young Child: Early Childhood Education

*Alice M. Meeker**

NURSERY SCHOOL

Tim Thomas stands in front of his apartment house waiting for the nursery school bus. He is a likable little chap in dungarees and sneakers, carrying a tiny box with holes punched in the top. The lid has been made secure by bands of scotch tape. There must be a gift inside for the teacher—Tim is guarding it so well! Soon the bus arrives and Tim climbs aboard still clutching his cardboard box. Forty-eight months is not a long time to have lived, but Tim is enjoying being four years old. Why?

When Mrs. Thomas enrolled him in nursery school her best friend was very critical. "He has many toys, the best of foods, and a loving home, and he walks with us in the park each day. What else does a child need?"

Mrs. Thomas reached for the brochure from Tim's nursery school and quoted: "These are the goals we hope to achieve with your child through providing the kind of environment and varied experience that:

* Alice M. Meeker is Special Consultant in Early Childhood and Elementary Education at Paterson State College, Wayne, New Jersey. She has contributed numerous articles to professional journals and has written several books, among them *I Like Children* and *Teachers at Work in the Elementary School.*

1. help him make a break from home and learn to live in a group setting
2. help him develop a joy in learning and experience success
3. help him develop self-control and responsibility
4. help him develop and make use of a four-year-old's creative ability."

Tim with a happy smile and with a praying mantis residing in his box is living proof that this nursery school is fulfilling its goals.

What Would a Day Be Like in a Nursery School?

The nursery school day is usually two to two and one half hours in length and might follow the sequence below:

Arrival   9:00–9:10
An informal time during which children put outer clothing on hooks and greet their friends.

Group Experience   9:10–9:20
A time to sing and share new material in art or science or a plaything.

Free Play   9:20–10:00
An opportunity for dramatic play, science or art activities, or playing with games, blocks, or books. Clean up is part of this.

Toilet Time   10:00–10:10
Wash up and get ready for—

Listening Time   10:10–10:20
A story is told by the teacher or a record is used.

Juice Time   10:20–10:35
Children pour juice, serve cookies, and clean up.

Music—Games—Dramatics   10:35–11:00

Outdoor Play   11:00–11:30
Best time for this—children remain fully dressed for—

Dismissal 11:30

Whatever the daily schedule of the nursery class—whether it be private or a Head Start class—we hope the teachers have in playing games, demonstrating with art media, or dramatizing tried always to work from left to right across the easel or chalkboard; that if lockers or other supplies are labeled or have students names on them, all printing will begin with a capital letter and all other letters in each word will be lower-case letters, as *Mary* not *MARY*. It is not too soon to realize that some nursery and kindergarten teachers can make problems for primary teachers when small items are overlooked.[1] Poor table manners developed during snack time, for instance, can make for future lunch problems in school.

The Nursery School Child

Perhaps as you read you are asking, "What are some of the characteristics of nursery-age children?" It is not easy to paint a word portrait of a four-year-old or a child of any other age. However, we might consider a few characteristics of these little persons. We use the term *persons,* for these children, though young, have distinct and fascinating personalities.

The *two-year-old* is friendly and easy to control.
The *three-year-old* is more willing to share and cooperate.
The *four-year-old* needs to be dealt with firmly. He is boastful, talks constantly, and shows vivid imagination.

One four-year-old whose sunburn was peeling remarked to his nursery school teacher, "I'm only four years old and I'm wearing out already!"

In summarizing the first portion of early childhood teaching,

---

[1] In preparing for reading, we want children to develop the habit of viewing from left to right. Similarly, since children will use manuscript writing in first grade, we want them to become accustomed to that form. Words having all letters capitalized establish a pattern that will later have to be unlearned.

we would hope that every child coming from nursery school classes, whether they be private, day-care centers, or government Head Start classes, would have been introduced to the most difficult arts all pupils must acquire:

1. The Art of Listening
2. The Art of Looking
3. The Art of Speaking
4. The Art of Asking Good Questions.

The child who has acquired these arts during nursery school years has a head start before the public school enrolls him.

To illustrate how well a four-year-old learns to listen, to look at a situation, to speak, and to parry a question, listen in on a group of four-year-olds.

The first boy states, "I remember when I was three years old. Do you?"

A little girl replies, "I remember when I was two years old. Do you?"

The third child, a boy, says, "I remember when I was only one year old. Do you?"

The fourth, a little girl typical of all girls, has the last word: "I remember when God said, 'Stand up while I pin your ears on.'"

You may have decided to teach four-year-olds and would like to know how one can evaluate such a teacher. The children do not read, write, or spell, but several evaluation scales have been compiled. The following list of areas of teacher performance, used to evaluate teachers in prekindergarten programs for disadvantaged children, illustrates the kinds of things we look for in a good nursery teacher:

1. Teacher interaction with pupils, in groups and individually.
2. Teacher interaction with aides and assistants.
3. Evidence of planning.
4. Techniques of classroom control.
5. Physical organization of the classroom.
6. Use of materials.
7. The preparation of special materials for a given purpose.

8. Sensitivity in terms of feedback.

9. Awareness of children's developmental status.

THE HEAD START PROGRAM[2]

One morning Miss Rutledge sat with her group of twelve four-year-olds who were devouring peanut butter sandwiches and orange juice. She served the snack early because several of the children came each day without breakfast. Suddenly, the door opened and a visitor entered. She looked over the situation and exclaimed, "How can you sit with so many peanut butter sandwiches?" What she really meant to imply was, "Aren't you bored with the situation?"

It would have been obvious to anyone professionally trained that Miss Rutledge was enjoying every minute spent in listening to her children as they exchanged confidences. As she and her aide replenished the sandwiches and refilled the cups with orange juice, she was amused by Chuckie's story to his seatmate, Juanita.

"Last night my mother came home from the hospital with a baby."

"Was it a brother?" inquired Juanita.

"No," replied Chuckie. "It's a girl. Besides she can't even talk." Then he added, "I told my father I'd play with her when she started to talk."

How typical of four-year-olds, thought Miss Rutledge. They are interested mostly in themselves. They like to hear stories which include their names and often enjoy playing by themselves. She also thought of Chuckie's home and its lack of even the necessities of life. Where could they possibly house one more child? There was very little interest in any of the family shown by Chuckie's father. No doubt his amusing remark about the baby's inadequacies went unnoticed by his shiftless father.

---

[2] The Head Start Program was authorized under the Economic Opportunity Act of 1964, discussed in Chapter 6. For a fuller discussion of the socially and culturally disadvantaged child, see Chapter 9.

How fortunate for Chuckie that there was a *Head Start* class to which he could come and unburden and learn.

Why a Head Start Program?

Recent research has indicated the value of attempting to give deprived children a "head start" in life:

> The more recent research has demonstrated that for children growing up under adverse circumstances the IQ may be depressed by a significant amount and that intervention at certain points (and especially in the period from ages three to nine) can raise the IQ by as much as ten to fifteen points.[3]

There are many other reasons for a Head Start class. Some children like Chuckie come from overcrowded, noisy homes where they have never learned to listen or to participate in normal conversation. They rarely sit down and eat together or go on trips outside their own neighborhood.

Juanita represents another problem which, if not alleviated, may cause more failure and less interest in school as she progresses. No English is spoken in her home or by her neighbors. The stores in which they shop are Spanish speaking. Until she came to Miss Rutledge's class, Juanita knew no English. Now she can request a toy by name, sing songs, ask for food, and carry on a conversation with her teacher and her classmates.

The Schedule

At this point, you may be wondering what a typical day's schedule would be like in a Head Start program. Here are two daily schedules: one for a three-hour program, the other for an all-day program. Naturally, these schedules must be flexible. The teacher who knows children's developmental patterns will shorten music period and lengthen story period if she deems it wise. *Any schedule* for this type of child must be extremely flexible.

---

[3] Benjamin S. Bloom, Allison Davis, and Robert Hess, *Compensatory Education for Cultural Deprivation* (New York: Holt, Rinehart and Winston, 1965), p. 12.

Three-Hour Schedule

1. *Work-play period* 60–90 minutes
   Spontaneous activity and planned activity.
2. *Quiet group activities* 40–50 minutes
   Toileting, washing.
   Music.
   Snack.
   Story.
   Rest.
3. *Outdoor play* 30–50 minutes (In bad weather the gymnasium is used.)
4. *Preparation for going home* 10 minutes (The end of the day should not be a frantic dash to get dressed.)
   At this time the following may take place:
   Toileting, washing.
   Pictures and books are readied to carry home.
   Any notes to parents are given to children.
   Wraps are put on.

All-Day Schedule

1. Breakfast, quiet play, listening to records, helping to get school ready. 7:00 A.M.–9:00 A.M.
2. A core period for work and play. 9:00 AM–12:00 noon
3. Luncheon. 12:00–12:45
4. Nap, rest, or some form of quiet time. 1:00 P.M.–3:00 P.M.
5. Outdoor play. 3:00 P.M.–5:00 P.M.
   Singing games.
   Dancing.
   Care of pets.
   Trips around neighborhood.
   Cooking. (They sometimes make jello, cranberry sauce, or apple sauce.)
6. Helping to close school for the day.

This program calls for lively adult planning, sometimes bringing in a guest to entertain the children. There should always be a happy closing.

Some Goals of the Head Start Class

Every well-organized Head Start class tries to do many things:

Curiosity is encouraged through exploration, discussions, and the use of smelling, touching, and looking to further arouse questions.

Language skills grow through the use of puppets, games, songs, puzzles, and playing together.

Discipline is fostered when a child is in a small group where he receives ample attention from an adult. In this atmosphere, his aggressions and destructive impulses frequently disappear.

A *good self-image*, so greatly needed by the disadvantaged child, is built in many ways but mostly by the teacher. Her smile, her touch, and the way she singles a child out for a word of commendation are sure to build a good image for the child. Just watch Peter when his teacher says, "You finished that difficult puzzle very quickly." His face will glow! Here is a teacher who knows that emotions are a powerful glue for making lessons stick.

The Head Start class does not always lessen the gap between advantaged and disadvantaged children. It can, however, prevent the gap from increasing before the child reaches kindergarten. The benefits derived should be seized by the kindergarten teacher at the beginning of the year.

Assignments for the Future Head Start Teacher

If you decide that you would like to teach in a Head Start program, here are a few preliminary assignments:

1. Observe the way a teacher interprets the program to a parent. A preschool class has no textbooks, there is much freedom of movement, and many activities take place at the same time. One father who worked at night spent the first hour visiting a Head Start class and then asked the teacher, "When does school really begin?"

2. Watch how the teacher, while still maintaining the role of leader, includes the teaching assistant or aide in the program.
3. Make a list of things the teacher might do and discuss with parents the evening they come for Open House.
4. Read several of the following magazine articles:

Bookbinder, Hyman. "Is America Waking Up?" *Childhood Education,* April, 1966, pp. 476–478.

Broman, Betty. "Parent's Reactions to Head Start Program," *Childhood Education,* April, 1966, p. 494.

Donovan, Hedley. "Fast Start for Head Start," *Time,* July 2, 1965, pp. 64–67.

Hechinger, Fred. "Head Start to Where?" *Saturday Review,* December 18, 1965, pp. 58–59.

Leven, Dorothy. "A Look at Project Head Start," *The Education Digest,* April, 1966, p. 8.

Ross, Irvin. "Head Start is a Banner Project," *The PTA Magazine,* March, 1966, pp. 20–24.

KINDERGARTEN

One crisp morning in December Miss L. noticed a young woman had opened the door to her kindergarten room and stood waiting with a toddler in a snow suit. In a hurried voice, she explained her first attempt at Christmas shopping had been a dismal failure. Pointing to the toddler she exclaimed, "He pulled things from the counters and cried most of the time."

Then came the surprise request. "May I leave him with you till three o'clock? His sister in sixth grade can take him home. I wouldn't ask any other teacher but, after all, kindergarten is just a waiting room till they can get into first grade."

The teacher explained that the building principal had to be consulted and closed the door quietly.

After her twenty-five pupils had departed, she asked herself this question: "Where do people acquire the notion that kindergarten is a place to wait?"

The Kindergarten Child

Sketching a portrait of a typical five-year-old is impossible, but a thumbnail sketch might point out a few characteristics of the average kindergarten pupil:

Characteristics of the five-year-old

1. Abounds in desire for physical activity.
2. Likes to be given responsibility.
3. Is eager for information *in small doses.*
4. Needs affection.
5. Has limited concept of time.
6. Is cooperative, sociable, stable.

Far from being a waiting room, the kindergarten is a beginning room—here the good backgrounds for English usage, for following sequence in a story, for noticing likenesses and differences in words are built. Unfortunately some kindergarten programs are still built around grandma's background where most of her ideas came from the teacher. Now the five-year-old has radio, television, and many other sources of ideas coming to him as soon as he can pull up his tiny rocker and look and listen to programs.

The Program and Goals of the Kindergarten

Though programs of kindergartens vary, most would include the following activities:

1. Work period.
2. Conference time.
3. Story time.
4. Music time.
5. Outdoor play.
6. Rest time.
7. Snack time.
8. Time to explore—indoor or outdoor exploration.

All of these activities have a purpose, for we are promoting current learning and developing readiness for future learning. We are helping these youngsters to learn to listen, to look, to speak, and to ask critical questions; we are helping them to discover more about the world in which they live; we are helping them to learn good habits of work, to be independent, to develop initiative, and to develop social and physical skills.

There has been much discussion in recent years as to whether formal reading instruction should be given in kindergarten. A full consideration of the question is beyond the scope of this discussion. It should be pointed out, however, that the real question is not whether children of this age *can* be taught to read (we know they can); rather, the question is whether children *should* be taught to read at such an early age. After referring to research on the question of reading in the kindergarten, Sue Moskowitz concluded:

> There is too much research evidence to be ignored showing that children not ready for formal [reading] instruction are liable to fail to learn, with resulting hostility towards education; and also that starting formal instruction early, at best, yields little or no advantage in later achievement, when non-early readers tend to catch up and even excel. In any case, it is up to educators to protect children from the swings of fashion in public opinion.[4]

Others disagree, but we do not have sufficient research to answer the question authoritatively at this time.

We want our children to develop the *art of listening* to stories. Some of the stories would be completed by the teacher; others would be left unfinished for the children to complete. The *art of looking* can be fostered by having children concentrate on likenesses and differences in pictures; by observing on field trips to nearby spots or the school yard; and by looking to see what is happening in a science experiment. Through telling events in the

[4] Sue Moskowitz, "Reading in the Kindergarten," *Pathways in Child Guidance*, A Publication of the Bureau of Child Guidance, Dr. Simon S. Silverman, editor, Board of Education, City of New York, Vol. 7, No. 2–3:9, March, 1965.

sequence in which they occurred, through the use of complete sentences, and through the use of distinct speech, youngsters can learn the *art of speaking.* With patience and proper teacher guidance, the *art of asking good questions* can be cultivated in these kindergarten boys and girls.

The horizons of children need to be widened so that they can include in the term *we* all children—Negro, white, yellow, and red-skinned. Use holiday celebrations to illustrate the likenesses and differences in the way various class members observe special days.

Permit some fantasy to creep into the everyday life of the kindergarten child. His love of fantasy and his frequent use of the phrase "I wonder" are clues to the charm one feels in teaching the five-year-old. A kindergarten teacher was recently given the opportunity to see how fantasy can even be extended experience in a small boy's life.

"I have a horse at home," said the five-year-old tenement dweller.

"Really," said the teacher. "I thought you lived on the fourth floor."

"Yes," said Joey, "I live on the fourth floor and I tie the horse to the door knob every morning."

Anxious to see Joey's fantastic powers, the teacher remarked, "I think I'll walk home with you at noon today and see this horse."

"Sorry, " said Joey. "He hit his head on the door knob and died this morning."

"Too bad," said the teacher while the others in the group looked puzzled.

The next day Joey began to tell about his horse.

One child said, "Didn't he die?"

"No," said Joey, "when I went home I gave him two aspirins and a glass of water and he got up and began to trot down the stairs."

Could you have enjoyed this saga with a class? Then, maybe, you would enjoy children who are still living partly in a world of fantasy in the kindergarten.

The Kindergarten Teacher

We want the kindergarten teacher to be and to know a great many things. For example, we want her to be a superb storyteller and a widely read person; we want her to know the needs of each child in her class and how to make each child feel that he is a part of and a *contributor* to the class; and we want her to be willing to experiment with new ideas and materials. She should know how to listen to children, to parents, and to the public.

The ability to tell stories well deserves special mention, for it is a most important skill, not only for kindergarten teachers but for all teachers. In Scotland's Holyrood Palace the tiles around the fireplaces were used as a background for storytelling before children's books were printed. Now that there are so many volumes of stories to tell children, it would seem wise if the kindergarten teacher would have, as her first goal, to become a fabulous storyteller. Would you enjoy viewing a program where the master of ceremonies held a tome before his face and read to you? Children must have the same sensation if the teacher must hold the book in front of her face because she does not know the story.

The kindergarten teacher, along with other teachers of early childhood education, enters a special world—the ever new world of the young. She can enhance this world of the child greatly: she can help to keep alive that "sense of wonder" of which Rachael Carson wrote:

> If a child is to keep alive his inborn sense of wonder . . . he needs the companionship of at least one adult who can share it, rediscovering with him the joy, excitement and mystery of the world we live in.[5]

PRIMARY GRADES

When Mrs. White sends the twins to the first grade, she has

[5] Rachael Carson, *The Sense of Wonder* (New York: Harper & Row, Publishers, 1956), p. 45.

definite ideas about what must happen. Jill, who is very mature
for six, must learn to read and write immediately, and so must
Jack, who is slow in speech and really not capable of listening for
any length of time. Her argument to any friend who dared to
question her would follow this pattern: "Of course they must stay
together; they are twins born at the same time and with the same
family background."

When Miss Black welcomes them to first grade, her thoughts
run in this pattern although she does not express them: "How well
Jill speaks. How quickly she notices the pictures around the
room. How well she holds the crayon. How quickly she falls in
line and keeps the beat with her triangle at music time. She is the
only one who notices that three of the dogs are black and one is
brown during the story told on the flannel board."

Jack greets the teacher as "Miss *Back*" and cries because he
cannot gallop or skip at rhythm time. Jack is a nice-looking child
and has a warm smile. He is like five or six others in the class.
Miss Black will work harder and give more time to Jack and his
group, but she will have problems with Jack's mother. Why? "Because he is a twin and taller than Jill and must take home a
reader the same day as Jill."

We give you this sketch so that you, as a student visiting primary grades, will note differences in children though they be the
same age with the same grandparents.

The Primary Teacher

Now for a short sketch of Miss Black, who represents the philosophy and goals of all good primary teachers. She has many
things planned for the twins and all her pupils but she has one
goal uppermost in her plans, her schedules, and her performance.
She is eager to hear from each child three magic words: "I can
read!" When she hears these and knows them to be true, she has
reached her greatest goal. She has also made the child more of an
individual. Now, he can explore books, charts, labels, signs. Now,
he can find out many things he has wondered about in science

such as What makes weather? How do we make certain sounds?
What will come from the cocoon?

He can read the signs and prices in the supermarket and experience early forms of mathematics. Best of all he can read his
favorite stories and write a letter to his favorite grandparent.

Miss Black knows that dropouts are made in the primary
grades, not in high school. Above all, Miss Black and all good primary teachers realize that a child thrives on *success*. As an illustration of how much this means to a primary teacher, we retell an
experience.

George had struggled with beginning reading. His patient
teacher had used every opportunity to make charts including
George's daily experiences such as:

George painted a good picture.
George played the drum today.
George brought a big shell.

Finally, the day came when George completed the first little
book. He carried it home with great pride.

The next morning he reported: "When my mother heard me
read she said, 'George, you growd a leaf today.' "

This mother had done what the teacher had hoped, even
though her grammar was incorrect. She had given George a feeling of *success*.

Teaching in the Primary Grades

You may at this point say, "I think I may enjoy teaching primary children more than four- and five-year-olds. Can you give
the portrait of a typical primary child?" This we cannot do, but
we think this acrostic on the word *children* gives many hints
about the young child in the elementary school.

Children are:
C – curious. They like to see, hear, feel, and taste things. They
     want answers to their questions.

H – hoarders. They collect stamps, shells, stones, bottle caps—
    anything!

I – individuals. Each must grow according to his pattern.

L – lively. They want to do and try things.

D – dreamers. They often say, "I wonder."

R – responsive. They like animals; they react quickly.

E – explorers. They like trips; they like to discover.

N – newsy. They want to know the *what* and *why* of things.

Whether you decide to teach a primary class where all the subjects are integrated or an ungraded primary, you should study and use this interpretation of the word *children.* You will learn from this list of characteristics how to plan for and with children. The materials needed, the trips, the questions to be asked and answered, and the calm atmosphere in the room are all here. The children will respond to your efforts.

The story of the boy who went home ecstatic about the plans for the next day illustrates this.

His mother asked why he was so delighted, and the third grader said, "Because we're going to cooperate with the other third grade."

When pressed further, he admitted he didn't know just what they were going to do; but his teacher's joy at the plan had been contagious.

If you should decide early in your college life that you want to teach in the area of early childhood, where every day is an adventure, here are some guidelines:

1. Play with children.
2. Eat with them and while eating discuss their favorite likes and greatest fears.
3. Watch people in buses, subways, airports—some of the parents will react as these people do.
4. Offer to accompany parents with small children on trips. Note the choices children make.
5. Listen to parents as they discuss their offspring and interpret their actions.

6. Listen to parents as they discuss schools and teachers.
7. Try to see master teachers at their craft.
8. If possible, attend a parent conference and note how a master teacher listens. Notice also how she remembers to relate at least one pleasant incident concerning the child before introducing more serious notes.

As a primary teacher, involve the parents of your children. Take the time, even though your parents are busy and burdened, to have them at least once a year as guests. Set up the room as the children see it each day. Let parents make something as evidence that they, too, have been in school. It may be a finger painting, a map, or a sketch.

Remember that these parents are members of your team! All communications, written or telephoned, represent you when they reach home. So, be certain that they are well phrased and courteous.

Homework Assignment for Early Childhood Teachers

We would like to give some "homework" for future teachers of early childhood education:

1. Collect
   a. 250 good, clear, colorful pictures.
   b. everything—shells, coins, dolls, stamps.
2. Learn to tell stories.
3. Learn to make quick decisions.
4. Learn how to make small experiences and trips worth while.
5. Learn to ask good questions and to *wait* to have them answered.
6. Learn the art of planning.
7. Learn the meaning of creativity.
8. Then follow the advice of an early New England settler who offered a student this recipe for improvement:
   a. read.
   b. read.
   c. read some more.

d. read anything.
e. read about everything.
f. read enjoyable things.
g. read things you yourself enjoy.
h. read and talk about it.
i. read very carefully some things.
j. read on the run most things.
k. don't think about reading but
l. just read.

If you decide to become a teacher of young children, here are some gifts we would bestow upon you to add to your professional education:

1. *An insatiable curiosity* so that, like Rudyard Kipling's Elephant Child, you will be the teacher who says "Let's find out" rather than tells the answers.

2. *A sense of wonder* so that you will ask who can find the first blade of grass in spring or the first colored leaf in fall; you will ask what shape snowflakes are and then take out a piece of black velvet and a magnifying glass so that the children can find out.

3. *A touch of sweet wind* so that you may laugh often with your class.

4. *The ability to always look poised and well dressed* regardless of personal woes. Recently, a primary teacher who usually wears drab colors and frequently wears a frown had this experience. She was going out to dinner and wore a bright colored dress, an attractive piece of jewelry, and a becoming hair-do. She probably smiled because of the prospect of a happy dinner party.

   A third grade boy looked at her as he entered the classroom and exclaimed, "Mrs. G., you look nice enough today to be a *substitute!*"

   What was he saying? If you plan to live five days a week with young children, ponder this anecdote.

5. We have saved your best gift till last. It is something we call

"mental springtime." If you have it, *every child* will be a new challenge and *every year* you teach will be exciting. Some teachers never enjoy it: master teachers never lose it!

SUGGESTED ACTIVITIES

1. Interview three youngsters who are in kindergarten or first grade and determine their attitudes toward school. If you are patient and approach the children properly, you should be able to secure quite a bit of information. Summarize your notes for class presentation.
2. View a film like "Skippy and the Three R's" (NEA) and note and discuss the good qualities of a primary teacher illustrated by such a film.
3. Prepare a report on the development of nursery or kindergarten education in this country.
4. Visit a nursery school, day nursery, or Head Start program and present to the class a report of your visit.
5. For a period of one week, view two or three of the television programs popular with young children. What did you think was valuable or not valuable for the children in these programs? Explain your views briefly in a written report.
6. With your instructor's approval, invite one of your professors in early childhood education to speak to the class about new developments in this field.
7. To recall the initial adjustment to school, it may be interesting for the class to discuss recollections of their first days of kindergarten.

SELECTED REFERENCES

Clark, Kenneth B. *Prejudice and Your Child.* Boston: Beacon Press, 1963. A discussion of prejudice with suggestions about how schools, community agents, and parents can deal with children's prejudices.

Crosby, Muriel. *Curriculum Development for Elementary Schools in a Changing Society.* Boston: D. C. Heath and Company, 1964. Section One, "The Child in the Elementary School," is particularly recommended. This section presents a description of the pressures upon the school and the reflection of these pressures upon the child, his family, and his community.

D'Evelyn, Katherine E. *Individual Parent-Teacher Conferences.* Revised edition. New York: Bureau of Publications, Teachers College, Columbia University, 1963. Gives valuable suggestions for organizing, conducting, and evaluating individual parent–teacher conferences.

Foster and Headley. Revised by Neith E. Headley. *Education in the Kindergarten.* Fourth edition. New York: American Book Company, 1966. A basic book in kindergarten education.

Heffernan, Helen, ed. *Guiding the Young Child: Kindergarten to Grade Three.* Second edition. Boston: D. C. Heath and Company, 1959. Helen Heffernan, a leader in the field of early childhood education, presents in this fine book guidelines for educating the young child.

Huey, J. Frances. *Teaching Primary Children.* New York: Holt, Rinehart and Winston, 1965. A good treatment of the primary school period of education. Deals with all curriculum areas. Part I, "Preparing for Primary Children," may be of particular interest.

Jenkins, Gladys Gardner, Shacter, Helen S., and Bauer, William W. *These Are Your Children.* Third edition. Chicago: Scott, Foresman and Company, 1966. An illustrative text on child development. Part Three, "The Preschool Years," and the primary-age section of Part Four, "The Primary and Middle Years," are directly related to the material discussed in this chapter of your text.

Lambert, Hazel M. *Early Childhood Education.* Boston: Allyn and Bacon, 1960. A thorough treatment of early childhood education. In addition to chapters on all curriculum areas, there are chapters on teaching the gifted child, teaching exceptional children, and working with parents.

Logan, Lillian M. *Teaching the Young Child: Methods of Preschool and Primary Education.* Boston: Houghton Mifflin Company, 1960. An excellent book that presents the characteristics of children at various ages and a program developed around these characteristics. In Part IV, "The Problems We Face," the author discusses common problems faced by classroom teachers.

Marshall, Sybil. *An Experiment in Education.* London: The Syndics of the Cambridge University Press, 1963. Mrs. Marshall recounts her eighteen years of teaching at a village school in England, where she developed a teaching method that employed the experimental approach. This is an inspirational book recommended for all elementary teachers.

Meeker, Alice M. *Teaching Beginners to Read*. New York: Holt, Rinehart and Winston, 1958. A handbook for teachers who are beginning to work with the art of teaching reading.

Pitcher, Evelyn Goodenough, and Ames, Louise Bates. *The Guidance Nursery School*. New York: Harper & Row, Publishers, 1964. A Gesell Institute book for teachers and parents that presents both research data and sound teaching methods in nursery education.

Salot, Lorraine, and Leavitt, Jerome E. *The Beginning Kindergarten Teacher*. Minneapolis: Burgess Publishing Company, 1965. Presents practical information for the beginning kindergarten teacher. For example, there is a complete chapter, Chapter III, on the first day of kindergarten.

Sowards, G. Wesley, and Scobey, Mary-Margaret. *The Changing Curriculum and the Elementary Teacher*. San Francisco: Wadsworth Publishing Company, 1961. An overview of the elementary curriculum. Chapter 10, "Listening and Reading: Receptive Language Arts," is illustrative of the comprehensive probing by the authors into the learning areas in the elementary curriculum.

3 Teaching in the Elementary School

Nowhere are the changes taking place in American education more evident than they are in the elementary school. The concern with school reorganization can be seen in the trend toward the middle school and the interest in the nongraded school. The curriculum reform movement has brought about changes not only in mathematics and science but in other areas of the curriculum as well. All that we know about human behavior and learning is now influencing what is to be learned by today's boys and girls and how it is to be taught. The objectives of education are being reexamined. Teachers are experimenting with new and cooperative ways to work in the team teaching format. There is much concern about the education of the disadvantaged minorities. Technology, with all its implications for change, is influencing teaching and learning through programed instruction, teaching machines, the application of computers to many educational tasks, and instructional television. Indeed, the elementary school is an exciting place in which to teach. It offers great challenge to those who will take up that work. Will you be one of those who will meet the challenge of the changing elementary school? Perhaps this chapter will help you to decide.

In a chapter-length treatment of elementary education, only certain topics can be included. What were believed to be the more important topics for those considering elementary teaching as a career have been selected for inclusion in this chapter. First, the objectives of the elementary school will be discussed so as to provide a basis for viewing the work of the elementary teacher. The program of the elementary school will be considered next, and an extended section will follow on teaching and learning in the elementary school. An exploration of the middle school and its implications for school organization will conclude the chapter. (The nongraded school, team teaching, and programed learning will be discussed separately in Chapter 7, and an overview of the socially and culturally disadvantaged student and his education will be found in Chapter 9, "Teaching All Children and Youth.")

THE OBJECTIVES OF THE ELEMENTARY SCHOOL

Many statements have been made about the purposes of the elementary school. The Report of the Mid-Century Committee on Outcomes in Elementary Education,[1] for example, outlines nine objectives of elementary education recommended by a committee of outstanding educators. The nine objectives are concerned with the broad areas of (1) physical development, health, and body care; (2) individual, social, and emotional development; (3) ethical behavior, standards, and values; (4) social relations; (5) the social world; (6) the physical world; (7) esthetic development; (8) communication; and (9) quantitative relationships. Five types of behavioral changes at three age-grade levels are examined for each of these areas. It is recognized, however, that youngsters differ and will not necessarily make consistent and uniform progress toward all of these objectives.

The Educational Policies Commission has stated that.

> The purpose which runs through and strengthens all other educational purposes—the common thread of education—is the development of the ability to think. . . . To say that it is central is not to say that it is the sole purpose or in all circumstances the most important,

[1] Nolan C. Kearney, *Elementary School Objectives* (New York: Russel Sage Foundation, 1953 .

but that it must be a pervasive concern in the work of the school.[2]

Surely, intellectual development is important and ought to be the central purpose of education, as the Commission points out. But it is not the *only* purpose of education. Teaching boys and girls how to think (though we are not even certain that we can teach someone how to think) is but one of the things the elementary school is trying to do, for the elementary school is concerned with many kinds of knowledge and understandings and with ideas, skills, appreciations, and attitudes. In short, it is concerned with developing the child in all areas for which it has responsibility. But for what should the school have responsibility?

In recent years, particularly, the school has been criticized for undertaking too many tasks. Things formerly done by the home, the church, or other agencies have been assigned to the school for one reason or another. President John H. Fischer of Teachers College, Columbia University, has said:

> Not only has the school been asked to offer more kinds of instruction for pupils, it is expected also to be a center for entertainment, civic development, charitable enterprises, and other more or less good works which, although they are conducted under the school's roof and in its stadium, can hardly be called educational.[3]

The school could do all things for children if it were the only agency concerned with the development of boys and girls. Obviously, this is not the case. Priorities, therefore, must be assigned to what the school is to do. President Fischer believes that we ought to

> . . . assign to the school the systematic development of intellectual, social, and vocational competence and to assign to other agencies the functions they can perform. Such a division of labor is no argument for a narrow or formalized curriculum. The good school is always concerned with the promotion of physical and mental health,

[2] Educational Policies Commission, *The Central Purpose of American Education* (Washington, D.C.: National Education Association, 1961), p. 12.
[3] John H. Fischer, "Schools Are for Learning," Paul Woodring and John Scanlon, eds., *American Education Today* (New York: McGraw-Hill Book Company, 1963), p. 3.

with productive and satisfying human relationships in a setting of moral and ethical values. Its teaching must be based upon the best that is known about human development and the nature of learning. It must make full use of the stimulating effects of group situations and should use as its tools every appropriate mechanical and electronic device.

It is not likely, however, that the school can produce the results it should in the specialized field of its own traditional activity if it must continue to expand or cannot reduce its obligations in other directions.[4]

The difficulty, though, is that the school is still being asked to take on new tasks—sex education, for example. As was pointed out above, people disagree on what tasks the school should assume, and sex education certainly illustrates the point. Many feel that this area of instruction is the province of the home and the church. Others believe that the home and church are not providing adequate sex education and that the school should give such instruction. Regardless of which position one takes on the question of sex education, one must face the fact that the school cannot do all things. Priorities must be established. Some agreement must be reached as to what are the most important things the school is to do.

What about the more specific question of the objectives of the elementary school? It is assumed here that the principal job of the elementary school is to promote sound development for children intellectually, physically, socially, and emotionally through a well-balanced program. In doing this, the school will help children to accomplish their *developmental tasks*. Professor Robert J. Havighurst of the University of Chicago describes these tasks:

The tasks which the individual must learn—the *developmental tasks* of life—are those things which constitute healthy and satisfactory growth in our society. They are the things a person must learn if he is to be judged and to judge himself to be a reasonably happy and successful person. *A developmental task is a task which arises at*

4 *Ibid.,* pp. 4–5.

about a certain period in the life of the individual, successful
achievement of which leads to his happiness and to success with
later tasks, while failure leads to unhappiness in the individual, dis-
approval by the society, and difficulty with later tasks.[5]

The developmental tasks of six- to twelve-year-old children, according to Dr. Havighurst, are the following:

1. Physical skill needed for ordinary games.
2. Wholesome attitudes towards self.
3. The ability to get along with age mates.
4. Appropriate masculine or feminine social roles.
5. Fundamental skills in reading, writing, and computing.
6. A scale of values, conscience, and morality.
7. An attitude toward social groups and institutions.
8. Personal independence.[6]

THE PROGRAM OF THE ELEMENTARY SCHOOL

As an elementary school teacher of the 1970's, the kinds of
things you teach will be very different from what you learned as
a student in the elementary school. The curriculum has been
changing and will continue to change, for knowledge is increasing at a tremendous rate today. It has been estimated that half of
what children now learn will become obsolete in less than a decade. Probably a good part of what you will be teaching a decade
from now is not yet known. Nevertheless, a view of some of the
developments in the elementary school program will give you an
idea of the currents of change within the curriculum.

The curriculum-reform movement began in the early 1950's
when scholars in the colleges and universities became concerned
with and involved in what the schools were teaching, particularly
in the fields of mathematics and science. Professor Jerold Zacharias of the Massachusetts Institute of Technology, through the
Physical Science Study Committee (PSSC), developed a new

[5] Robert J. Havighurst, *Developmental Tasks and Education* (Chicago:
The University of Chicago Press, 1948), p. 6. By permission of David Mc-
Kay Co., Inc.
[6] *Ibid.*, pp. 33–62.

course in high school biology. Educational Services, Inc., (ESI) was established as a nonprofit organization in 1958 to handle the new high school physics program. ESI moved into other projects —the Elementary Science Study project, for example—and became an important group in the curriculum-reform movement. The merger of ESI with IEI (Institute for Educational Innovation) to form EDC (Educational Development Center, Inc.) may have produced the most influential group in curriculum reform in the country. It has even been referred to as "the General Motors of curriculum reform."[7]

Another influential figure has been Professor Jerome S. Bruner, the noted psychologist of Harvard University. In 1960 he published *The Process of Education,* a book that reported on the famous Woods Hole Conference of scientists, educators, and psychologists called together to discuss the improvement of the science curriculum. This report[8] brought educators and the public an understanding of the importance of structure in the organization of school subjects. The concept of structure in a subject or discipline is not new; what is new is the emphasis being given to identifying the structure of a discipline and to teaching that discipline on the basis of its structure. As Professor Bruner says:

> The new curriculums . . . are based on the fact that knowledge has an internal connectedness, a meaningfulness, and that for facts to be appreciated and understood and remembered, they must be fitted into the internal meaningful context.[9]

There is disagreement, of course, on the use of structure for organizing school subjects. Professors Saylor and Alexander believe that "the use of structure as a basis for organizing the disciplinary subjects at the elementary school level is very limited."[10] Further-

[7] James D. Koerner, "EDC: General Motors of Curriculum Reform," *Saturday Review,* August 19, 1967, p. 56.
[8] Jerome S. Bruner, *The Process of Education* (Cambridge, Mass.: Harvard University Press, 1960)
[9] Jerome S. Bruner, "Structures in Learning," *NEA Journal,* 52:27, March, 1963.
[10] J. Galen Saylor and William M. Alexander, *Curriculum Planning for Modern Schools* (New York: Holt, Rinehart and Winston, 1966), p. 183.

more, some subjects, such as industrial arts, homemaking, and business, do not fit within the recognized disciplines. There is also a question of whether disciplinary subjects organized on their structure are the best kind of material for students of low academic ability.

Learning by discovery and inquiry is a basic part of the new curriculum plans. Students are to uncover principles for themselves rather than simply to get "the right answer"; students are led to ask fundamental questions and to find the answers from their own observations. Professor Bruner ties the process of discovery in with the concept of structure:

> Discovery, whether by a schoolboy going it on his own or by a scientist, is most often a matter of rearranging or transforming evidence in such a way that one is now enabled to go beyond the evidence to new insights. Discovery involves the finding of the right structure, the meaningfulness.[11]

Learners are to be active, not passive; the emphasis is on finding out, not telling.

Elementary school science does present problems today, not the least of which is that many teachers just are not properly prepared to teach the subject. It is fine to have boys and girls observing and experimenting in science, but they do need a teacher who knows science well enough to direct their learning. Just as there are those who are concerned about the lack of knowledge in science of some teachers and many students, there are those who are equally concerned about what they believe to be the overemphasis on science today. It must be admitted, though, that much of the impact of the "new science" has been felt in the secondary school, not in the elementary school.

Nearly everyone has heard or read about the "new math," which is now pretty well established in the schools. The most widely used materials are those developed by the School Mathematics Study Group (SMSG), though a number of groups worked on new mathematics programs such as The Greater Cleveland

[11] Jerome S. Bruner, "Structure in Learning," p. 27.

Mathematics Program, the University of Illinois Arithmetic Project, and Stanford University's Institute for Mathematical Studies in the Social Sciences. Not only does the new mathematics present new content, it is also a new approach to teaching and learning mathematics in the elementary school. Concepts are stressed rather than rote memorization of procedures; effort is made to have youngsters understand an operation, not merely perform it. The structure of mathematics is emphasized and much use is made of deductive reasoning and proof. A discovery approach is utilized. Content formerly taught in the high school is now taught in the elementary school.

There have been troubles with the new math. Some schools have gone off on crash programs, sometimes with almost disastrous results. There was not sufficient preparation, nor was the shift gradual, sound, or well thought out. Pupils were not ready, teachers were not ready, and parents added more gray hair in attempting to help their youngsters with math homework. Though many inservice programs have been conducted to enable teachers to secure the necessary knowledge, there are still elementary teachers not sure of themselves in the new mathematics. Some have proposed that specialists are needed in the elemetary school to teach mathematics (and science as well). Perhaps this will become a generally accepted idea. At any rate, more preparation in the area of mathematics education would be of value to the prospective teacher.

Reading, the heart of the elementary program, has received much attention. There are now so many approaches to reading that it would require quite a bit of space just to describe them. So far, it seems that there is no one best way to teach reading; each method has its merits and each learner his particular needs. An illustration of a newer approach to reading is The Initial Teaching Alphabet (ITA), developed by Sir James Pitman in England. ITA is an augmented alphabet of forty-four characters: twenty-four resembling the letters in the usual alphabet and twenty for sounds not covered in the usual alphabet. When the child has mastered beginning reading through the use of ITA, he makes the transition to reading material in the regular alphabet. Advocates of the method claim that ITA not only helps in beginning reading but also in other areas of the language arts—writing, spelling, and speaking. Though ITA is an interesting approach to beginning reading, it is too soon to make a final judgment. More research over a longer period of time is needed.

Attempts have been made to develop reading materials that are more representative of our urban populations. It is very difficult for a child to identify with the reader's "Dick" and "Jane," who live in a fine, comfortable suburban house with much-interested middle-class parents, when he lives in a crowded, dilapidated tenement in the inner city with a working mother and no father. Multi-ethnic editions of readers picture a variety of children, not just white children. Urban situations are brought into the stories. Through this type of material, all children, not just children of the minorities in the slums, can be introduced to the various kinds of people and life styles that make up American society.

The social studies curriculum reform has been later in developing than the reforms in mathematics and science. However, some new materials are now in use and others are being developed. As in other areas of the curriculum, stress is being placed on inquiry and discovery. Students are working not just with textbooks but with source materials as well. Instead of reading about treaties, for example, pupils make use of true copies of them. Texts themselves are more readable and interesting. More attention is being given to other peoples of the world and to the role of the Negro in American history. There is increased emphasis on subject matter and on the methods of the social sciences.

In the primary grades, the local community is still studied (food, shelter, clothing, and community workers, for example), but attempts are being made to move beyond the study of the immediate community to a wider world and to expand the horizons of children. Economics education is even being offered in the lower grades. Better ways are being considered of teaching citizenship so as to make it less the "bore" that many students have found it to be. One writer has characterized much of the teaching of citizenship through social studies as " . . . sentimental, contrived, self-conscious, and ineffective."[12] Much is going on in the social studies and much more is to come.

Among the many new things at the Nova schools in Fort Lauderdale, Florida, is the use of academic games. Democracy, for instance, is not studied from a book but by games that require solutions arrived at by democratic means. The Nova Academic Games Project, with financial assistance from the Ford Foundation and the U.S. Office of Education, is attempting to develop and refine academic games, which are intricately designed methods of teaching subject matter in a pleasurable way. The games range quite a bit in their complexity, but all are based upon competition to help students to understand and use new knowledge. It is believed that the attitude of students toward learning can be improved through the use of such games. Some examples of the games are Equations, a mathematics game that can be used in elementary and secondary school; WFF'N Proof, a game of modern logic, versions of which are suitable for the six-year-old on up through to the adult; and The Life Career Game, which is used in grades 7 through 12 to simulate the planning of a person's life involving decisions on education, occupation, family life, and leisure-time activities.

Many of the schools that got on the bandwagon of foreign language in elementary school (FLES) in the last decade have had second thoughts. Of course there are benefits to teaching a foreign language to children. It is, for instance, easier to learn a second language while a child if that language is properly taught. Too often, however, the foreign language was simply "put in" the elementary program as a kind of decoration. It was nice for school people to be able to say to visitors that the children were learning French. Many parents were equally pleased by such instruction. The fact that there were few qualified teachers, that there was little "instruction," and that there was no continuity was

[12] Ralph C. Preston, "The Social Studies: Nature, Purpose and Signs of Change," Maurie Hillson, ed., *Elementary Education: Current Issues and Research* (New York: The Free Press, A Division of the Macmillan Company, 1967), p. 91.

not so well advertised. Even where there were good foreign-language programs, there was still the problem of fitting the new instruction into the total program. The elementary school already has a program that is quite full, and something has to "give" to make room for foreign language. No doubt there are children who could benefit much from FLES, but one wonders if the time of most children could not be put to better use.

Outdoor education or school camping is being experimented with by some schools. The purpose is to provide opportunities for children to spend some time in a special outdoor environment that is conducive to good learning and group living. Usually a class is taken as a whole to spend one week in a camp owned by the school or rented from a public or private agency. Here, the boys and girls are given a guided experience in outdoor living. Regular teachers are aided by special counselors or resource persons whose function is to enrich the educational experience provided for the children. Outdoor education is not just recreation, it is an expansion of the school program, for it provides

> . . . learning by direct experience, enrichment of the traditional curriculum, opportunity for individual growth and experiences of working with a group, and occasions for the development of worthy attitudes toward work, conservation of natural resources, and protection of the rights of others. The camping experience provides plenty of opportunity for formal and informal learning activities.[13]

Obviously, outdoor education is not for all schools. Many schools in or near rural areas can furnish this kind of education in their own setting. Other schools do not have such facilities conveniently available; still others cannot afford this kind of program. For the relatively few schools now involved in such a program, though, outdoor education does offer many benefits.

Art, physical education, and music are discussed in Chapter 8 in connection with teaching careers in these fields. There is still merit, however, in mentioning here that these subjects should not be considered as "extras" but as important parts of the elementary

[13] Kenneth H. Hansen, *Public Education in American Society,* Second edition (Englewood Cliffs, N.J.: Prentice-Hall, © 1963), p. 187.

school program. Every boy and girl should have the opportunity for experiences in these areas of education on a regular basis in the elementary school.

This discussion of the program of the elementary school has of necessity been but an overview. Nevertheless, it may have indicated to you the wide range of knowledge needed by one who wishes to teach in the elementary school. Perhaps it has also given you some idea of the many changes taking place in the curriculum. This change, which is really always part of a good school and its program, is what makes elementary teaching interesting, challenging, and exciting.

TEACHING AND LEARNING IN THE ELEMENTARY SCHOOL

Quite obviously teaching and learning are the principal activities taking place in the elementary school; not quite so obvious is the fact that these are complex processes. Neither teaching nor learning is simply a matter of "common sense." There are theories of learning, but how people really learn is not yet fully understood. Subsequent course work will bring you a fuller knowledge of both teaching and learning. In the limited discussion that follows, only certain basic points and newer directions can be presented.

More emphasis is being placed on learning today than on teaching, for teachers are seen more as guides to learning than as dispensers of knowledge. Most of the curriculum reforms discussed above focus on a discovery approach to learning in which the student probes, questions, and solves problems. This is in contrast to a kind of learning that involved much drill and memorization. Students now are active in the learning process, not passive, and learning is going beyond the classroom to make use of other people and areas in the school, the home, and the community. The modern teacher, with more devices and materials to guide pupil learning than ever before, works with small groups and individuals much of the time.

Learning is more than the acquisition of knowledge and skill;

learning involves modification of behavior. A student may learn from another student, from something at home, from something on the way to school—in short, the student may learn from many kinds of experiences, not simply those provided by his teacher or school. But learning does involve *experience*. The learner must be involved with what he is to learn; he must use information in some way that has meaning for him. Thus, learning is an *active* process.

Learning involves the whole person, the whole organism, and not merely mental development. The stage of development of the learner, therefore, is most significant, for learning must be adjusted to the learner's present stage of development. Though all children go through certain developmental stages, they do not do so at the same rate or time; though all have potential for growth, and thus for learning, not all have the same potential. Each child is different from every other child. Hence the concept of *individual differences*, a concept central to learning. In view of this concept, it is very difficult to say that there is any *one* best way for all to learn or, for that matter, *one* best way to teach. A variety of approaches to teaching and learning is probably best, though ideally every child should be taught in the way that is best for him.

A child is his family, his friends, his neighborhood. He is influenced by them and reflects their values. If a good learning situation is to be established, the teacher must know not only the child but also the environment from which he comes. Nowhere is this more apparent than in the case of children from lower-class homes who, most often, are taught by middle-class teachers. Many of these teachers know little of the background of such children. As a result, lower-class children frequently find difficulty in functioning well in school. The ways in which teachers approach them, the values held and promulgated by their teachers, and the atmosphere and structure of the typical classroom are too different from what the children know or are accustomed to. Knowledge of the learner, therefore, is essential to effective teaching.

If the pupil is to learn, he must see something of value to himself in what is to be learned. He must be motivated to learn. (A good part of your job as teacher is to motivate children to learn.) There must be some purpose or goal that the learner can see as useful and realistic. As the learning proceeds, the pupil should see results, he should have knowledge of his progress. Nothing succeeds like success. Thus learning should be structured so that the learner does experience success, certainly more success than failure. It is true that one learns by his mistakes, but a learning situation that produces too much failure leads the learner to become discouraged and disinterested.

What a child thinks of himself and how he feels generally influence his learning. It is difficult to learn if you come to school without breakfast as many impoverished children do. It is difficult to learn if you are emotionally upset about some problem. It is difficult to learn if you do not have some sense of security, some sense of belonging. It is difficult to learn if you do not think you are a worthwhile person, if you do not have a good self-concept. It is your responsibility as teacher to help your pupils to feel more adequate as persons and to develop a sense of security and a feeling that they belong, at least in your classroom.

As a teacher, be sure to make your classroom a good place for students to come to. Make it a place that is alive, vital, and interesting. Make it a place where children feel comfortable, and plan so that they can get the most out of each day. Know your class as individuals and as a group, and be aware of what is going on in your classroom. Have centers of interest for the children around the room—for example, a science table and a classroom library of appropriate books. Be sure that you have good bulletin boards and that they are changed frequently. (Santa Claus should be gone by January.) Pace your teaching so that it does not "drag." Make use of variety in your lessons and look at the children frequently when you are teaching. Be able, on occasion, to put down the book and tell a story to your class. Have a purpose for each thing you do and plan it well.

The intellectual, social, and emotional climate of the classroom greatly affect learning. Without repeating the points made in Chapter 1, emphasis is again called to the importance of a good classroom climate. Your primary function is not to give therapy to students; your primary function is to teach. But you do want to be certain that your classroom is a mentally healthy one for children. There is no place in the classroom for excessive tension. There is no place in the classroom for sarcasm and ridicule. There is no place in the classroom for vindictive punishment.

Gear your teaching to the maturity level of your pupils. The amount and kind of learning that children are ready for does vary with their stage of development. You cannot expect primary grade children to sit through a two-hour lesson, to give an extreme example. Upper-grade students do not want to be treated as "babies." You should know the approximate length of the attention span of your children. You should know that children need to move about at intervals, that they need variety, and that they need activities suited to their developmental stage. Children, however, do need the security of a general routine. They need to know what to expect and what is to come next. This does not mean that you cannot deviate from your schedule. It does not mean that you cannot take advantage of a sudden interest by the children in a topic that comes up incidentally in the lesson.

Sound planning will overcome so many problems for you. Most discipline problems, for instance, can be traced to poor planning. Dorothy G. Petersen, in summing up the underlying causes of "normal" group misbehavior, listed the following factors: ". . . (1) uninteresting teaching-learning situations, (2) unwise academic pacing, (3) unhealthy classroom environment, (4) lack of organization, and (5) weak teaching personality."[14] With the exception of weak teaching personality the other causes of misbehavior listed could largely be eliminated through wise planning. Children without things to do, particularly things that interest them,

[14] Dorothy G. Petersen, *The Elementary School Teacher* (New York: Appleton-Century-Crofts Division of Meredith Publishing Company, 1964), p. 123.

will frequently present behavior problems. Have a variety of activities for pupils, therefore. If you are working with a reading group, do not forget about the rest of the class. Plan other work for them to do. Perhaps the arrangement could be that when the children finish the regular work you have assigned for them to do (while you are working with the separate reading groups), they can then go on to work on things in which they have a special interest. Please do not rely heavily on the use of workbooks to keep your students occupied, though. So much of this kind of work is simply "busy work" and, thus, is of little or no value.

Much of the homework typically assigned by elementary teachers also comes under the category of "busy work." Admittedly, homework is a controversial topic on which opinions differ widely. There are some who would abolish homework completely, but the major arguments are over the type and the amount of homework to be assigned. The research done on homework, however, does not lead to any definite conclusions.[15] It cannot be argued, therefore, that homework positively results in increased achievement for all students. Nor can it be argued, on the basis of research, that homework is of no value.

The schools have gone through various stages with regard to homework practices. Early in this century, it was believed that homework played an important part in disciplining the mind. In the 1930's, there was criticism of the excesses in length of assignments, routine memorization, and the use of homework for punishment. (We have enough trouble getting students interested in learning without instilling negative attitudes by using learning as a device for punishment.) There was a movement in the 1940's to do away with homework, especially in the elementary grades, which led to a view by many educators in the 1950's that homework should be optional. The launching of the first Sputnik in 1957, which helped to bring about an emphasis on subject matter

---

[15] National Education Association, Research Division, *Homework*, Research Summary 1966-S2 (Washington, D.C.: the Association, 1966), p. 4.

in the schools, had its effect on homework. Homework was seen as a way of achieving academic excellence.[16]

Current practices seem to reflect all of the stages through which thought on homework has passed. Assignments that stress routine memorization are still given by some teachers. More teachers, one would hope, are giving homework assignments that have purpose and are of interest to the child. Still other teachers assign no homework at all. Schools that have adopted homework policies, and this is to be recommended, seem to advocate that little or no homework be given in grades 1 to 3; that homework in grades 4 to 6 range from 30 to 45 minutes in length a night; and that grades 7 and 8 have homework that takes no more than an hour or an hour and a half to complete. Naturally, practice varies from school to school and even from teacher to teacher within a particular school.

It must be remembered in considering homework that children have more opportunity today for supervised study in school. They can begin and perhaps complete their work under the guidance of the teacher in an atmosphere conducive to study. At home, they do not always find such an atmosphere or such expert assistance. Furthermore, there are a great many things in a child's life besides homework. He needs time to play and relax from school work. He needs time to pursue such things as scouting, church activities, music lessons, and hobbies. He needs time to be a child. Remember too, that homework is designed for students, not parents. Though parents can help in many ways (by providing a quiet place to study, for example), there is little value in parents doing the homework for the child. The confusion that can result from this for the child is easily seen in "new math" assignments on which many a parent has put in a long evening to no avail.

Ideally, homework assignments should be given individually on the basis of each student's needs. In reality, however, not many teachers have the time for this. Still, some attempt at individualization of assignments should be made. Be sure that students understand the what, the why, and the how of assignments—what is

[16] *Ibid.*, p. 3.

to be done, why it is to be done, and how it is to be done. Devise homework that bears some relationship to what has been going on in class, and vary the kind of homework you give. Take the time to look at homework submitted. If students have put time into doing the assignment, you should go over their work. Finally, put thought into planning assignments. Make them valuable for the student, and do not give homework simply for the sake of giving homework. The student has better things to do with his time than do unnecessary homework, and you can be better occupied than correcting work that was not necessary in the first place.

THE MIDDLE SCHOOL

Change is taking place in school organization. There is much discussion of a new form of organization involving a middle school. The term *middle school* is used with frequency not only in the professional literature but also in popular periodicals and the press. The middle school could be defined as a unit of organization between the elementary school and the high school, but such a definition would only be a beginning point. The grade levels included in this new unit vary: some would include grades 7, 8, and 9, now found in the typical junior high school; some would include grades 6, 7, and 8; and others would place grades 5 through 8 in the middle school.

A good part of the interest in the middle school has come about because of dissatisfaction with the junior high school as it has come to function in American education. A number of educators believe the original purpose of the junior high school and its special functions (discussed at length in the next chapter) have been altered radically; they believe that the junior high school has become simply an appendage of the high school rather than a special institution for the education of early adolescents. Some indication of the extent of the dissatisfaction can be seen in the title of an article by A. H. Rice that appeared in the *Nation's Schools* for November, 1964: "What's Wrong with Junior Highs? Nearly Everything."

Professor Samuel H. Popper considers the junior high school as the middle school and states the issue in this way:

> What over the years we have come to know as the Junior High School is institutionally America's Middle School. What is at issue now in professional dialogue is not whether there shall be a junior high school or a middle school, a semantic distinction without a difference, but rather which grades are functionally appropriate for this unit of public school organization.[17]

Professor Popper's view is that the middle school is basically a school for educating early adolescents. Donald H. Eichhorn, on the other hand, sees the middle school as an institution for educating transescents—those in that period of human development ". . . which begins in late childhood prior to the onset of puberty and extends through the early stages of adolescence."[18] Thus Eichhorn would include in the middle school grades 6 through 8. He believes that physical maturation is occurring at an earlier chronological age than it used to and that

> . . . this trend has developed to the point where transescents with similar physical maturation characteristics are now being educated at two separate organizational levels—the sixth grade, considered elementary, and the seventh and eighth grades associated with the junior high school.
>
> Although the current 6–3–3 grade organization effectively met the needs of youngsters in the earlier decades of this century, it no longer relates realistically to the physical characteristics of transescents.[19]

Still another writer, Dr. M. Ann Grooms, sees the middle school as serving students ten to fourteen years of age,[20] students who

---

[17] Reprinted by permission of the publisher, from Samuel H. Popper, *The American Middle School: An Organizational Analysis* (Waltham, Mass.: Blaisdell Publishing Company, A Division of Ginn and Company, 1967), p. xi.

[18] Donald H. Eichhorn, *The Middle School,* The Library of Education (New York: The Center for Applied Research in Education, 1966), p. 107.

[19] *Ibid.,* p. 102.

[20] M. Ann Grooms, *Perspectives on the Middle School* (Columbus, Ohio: Charles E. Merrill Books, 1967), p. 4.

would ordinarily fall within the range of grades 5 through 9. The reader can see then that there is quite a difference of opinion as to just which grades belong in the middle school.

New York City is changing its form of school organization, which now incorporates the junior high school in a 6–3–3 pattern, to 4–4–4 pattern—four years of elementary school, four years of middle school, and four years of high school. Middle schools are in operation or in the planning stages in many other places, including the cities of Portland, Oregon, and Pittsburgh. Many of those responsible for developing middle schools approach the new organization on educational grounds. They believe, for example, that a four-year high school makes more sense now because attendance is usually required by law until age sixteen. (Before the junior high school was started early in this century, many students were dropping out at the end of the eight-year elementary school. By establishing junior high schools including ninth grade, it was hoped that students would remain in school longer and go on to high school.) And they believe that due to earlier development ninth graders are really more suited to the high school and its programs. They likewise believe that many fifth and sixth graders can benefit more from a middle school attuned to their special needs than they can from the usual elementary school environment and program.

Other advocates of the middle school are attempting to solve a social problem with a new school organization. The problem they are attempting to solve is *de facto* racial segregation, especially in urban areas. Neighborhood elementary schools tend to have enrollments that mirror residence patterns. Thus ghetto areas have elementary schools that are predominantly segregated. Since junior and senior high schools draw from a wider attendance area, they can have student bodies that are more integrated. By reorganizing and establishing middle schools within a 4–4–4 pattern, however, students are brought out of the elementary school two years earlier into the middle school. With the wider attendance area of the middle school and an open enrollment policy (a policy that allows students to enroll in a school of their choice, if space is available) racial integration is facilitated.[21] Professor Popper sees this use of the middle school " . . . more as a temporary escape from the pressures of a deeply rooted social problem than as a solution."[22] He further believes that the middle school will be diverted from its legitimate goal if it is used simply as a device to facilitate racial integration. Though integration of the schools is a high priority item in American education, Popper states that

> . . . school boards weaken the institution of public school education when they fulfill one societal obligation at the expense of another. Such is the case when the pursuit of racial integration is allowed to divert the middle school from its legitimate goal.[23]

What the future holds for the middle school remains to be seen. Dialogue is certain to continue. But the outcome of such dialogue is bound to affect the junior high school, the institution to which considerable attention will be given in the next chapter.

SUGGESTED ACTIVITIES

1. Arrange with your instructor to spend a day observing in an elementary school. If possible, visit several classes—perhaps a first, third, fifth, and sixth grade. Prepare a report of the teaching and learning activities you observed in these classes.
2. Prepare a report on the changes taking place in an area of the elementary school curriculum of special interest to you.
3. Give an illustration of poor classroom discipline from your experience. How did the teacher contribute to the problem? How would you have handled the situation?
4. Write a report in which you discuss five kinds of homework assignments that would be of value to pupils in the elementary school.
5. Select a committee to prepare and present a debate on the question of whether or not the public schools should provide sex education.
6. With your instructor's approval, invite an elementary school principal to speak to the class about the objectives of his school and some

---

[21] Popper, *op. cit.*, p. 294.
[22] *Ibid.*, pp. 294–295.
[23] *Ibid.*, pp. 295–296.

of the ways in which he and his staff are attempting to achieve these objectives.

7. After consulting the current literature on the middle school, outline in a report for class presentation the major elements of a good middle school program.

8. Identify and discuss the three objectives you would stress most as an elementary teacher.

SELECTED REFERENCES

Bruner, Jerome S. *The Process of Education.* Cambridge, Mass.: Harvard University Press, 1960. Emphasizes the importance of structure in learning as well as readiness for learning and intuitive and analytic thinking.

Burton, William H. *The Guidance of Learning Activities.* Third edition. New York: Appleton-Century-Crofts, 1962. A comprehensive text. See especially Part I, "The Principles of Learning," and Part II, "The Learner and the Teacher."

Collier, Calhoun C., and others. *Teaching in the Modern Elementary School.* New York: The Macmillan Company, 1967. Takes the position that teaching is a total process, not a series of separate acts. Chapters deal with such topics as providing for individual differences (Chapter 8), measurement and evaluation (Chapter 12), and reporting pupil progress (Chapter 13).

Eichhorn, Donald H. *The Middle School.* The Library of Education. New York: The Center for Applied Research in Education, 1966. Presents the concept of a middle school in a 5–3–4 pattern for transescents—those in the developmental stages of late childhood through to the early stage of adolescence.

Fleming, Robert S., ed. *Curriculum for Today's Boys and Girls.* Columbus, Ohio: Charles E. Merrill Books, 1963. A valuable source book for the prospective teacher. Takes the point of view that learning must be active and real and that such learning must be carefully planned.

Goodlad, John I., and Anderson, Robert H. *The Nongraded Elementary School.* Revised edition. New York: Harcourt, Brace & World, 1963. A classic statement of the philosophy and operation of the nongraded school. Comprehensive bibliography.

Grooms, M. Ann. *Perspectives on the Middle School.* Columbus, Ohio:

Charles E. Merrill Books, 1967. Presents a somewhat brief description of the middle school involving a nongraded concept and team teaching. The author discusses the students, staff, purposes, program, and future of the middle school.

Hilson, Maurie, ed. *Elementary Education: Current Issues and Research.* New York: The Free Press, A Division of the Macmillan Company, 1967. A group of readings which surveys recent research findings, evaluations of ongoing experiments, new ideas, and commentary on persistent issues in elementary education. Selections on such topics as reading, nongradedness, computer-based instruction, and team teaching.

Meeker, Alice M. *I Like Children.* Evanston, Ill.: Row, Peterson and Company, 1953. The author puts forth a philosophy about children that has value for all teachers.

Meeker, Alice M. *Teachers at Work in the Elementary School.* Indianapolis, Ind.: The Bobbs-Merrill Company, 1963. A most interesting and practical book. For example, there is a chapter on classroom management (Chapter 2) and one that answers such basic questions as "What can I do with the slow reader?" and "How can I get along with parents?" (Chapter 11).

Petersen, Dorothy G. *The Elementary School Teacher.* New York: Appleton-Century-Crofts, Division of Meredith Publishing Company, 1964. A practical text on teaching in the elementary school. Suggests materials to use and where to secure them. Chapter 13, "Meeting Persistent Problems," is particularly useful.

Popper, Samuel H. *The American Middle School: An Organizational Analysis.* Waltham, Mass.: Blaisdell Publishing Company, A Division of Ginn and Company, 1967. An advanced, analytical treatment of this complex subject. The need for a middle school and the special function it fulfills in educating the early adolescent are considered.

Ragan, William B. *Modern Elementary Curriculum.* Third edition. New York: Holt, Rinehart and Winston, 1966. A good overall reference. Curriculum foundations, curriculum organization, and all curriculum areas are discussed. Many illustrations and specific suggestions are given.

Sharp, Evelyn. *A Parent's Guide to the New Mathematics.* New York: E. P. Dutton Company, 1964. Written especially for parents, this book explains the "mysteries" of the new mathematics being introduced into American schools.

Thomas, George I., and Crescimbeni, Joseph. *Individualizing Instruction in the Elementary School*. New York: Random House, 1967. A text based on the hypothesis that ". . . learning must be continuous and that children must have opportunities to progress at their own rates of speed." Chapter 7, "Recognizing the Need for Creativity," is of particular interest.

Wolf, William C., Jr., and Loomer, Bradley M. *The Elementary School: A Perspective*. Chicago: Rand McNally & Company, 1966. This text focuses on three main topics: "the evolving nature of the elementary school's purposes, organization, curriculum and methodology; characteristics of the children who attend the school; and the staff that operates it."

4 Teaching in the Secondary School

It is difficult to discuss teaching in *the* secondary school, for in reality there are many kinds of secondary schools. You may teach in a large, comprehensive high school, a small high school with a limited program, a technical high school, or a special high school, such as a high school of commerce or science. It may be organized as a four-year high school, a three-year junior high school and a three-year senior high school, a six-year junior-senior high school, or a two-year junior high and a four-year senior high school. The school may be an urban, a suburban, or a central rural school, each of which has its own special problems. As many as 70 percent of the graduates may be going on to college, or as few as 25 percent may go on to higher education. The dropout rate may be quite low or as high as 60 percent. Various combinations of these ingredients make up the variety of secondary schools in America.

Speaking statistically, however, most high schools are small (under 300 students),[1] but most students go to larger schools.[2] Furthermore, most students attend some form of junior high school.[3]

[1] Edmond A. Ford and Virgil R. Walker, *Statistics of Education in the United States: 1958–59*, U.S. Office of Education E-20032-59 (Washington, D.C.: Government Printing Office, 1961), p. 7.
[2] *Ibid.*, pp. 12–13.
[3] *Ibid.*, pp. 8–9.

The national dropout rate is about 30 percent, which means that 70 percent of high school students will be graduated. About 28 percent of those graduated will go on to college, with another 7 percent going to some noncollegiate, post-secondary school.

Let's not get lost in statistics, however. Attention is to be focused on *teaching* in the secondary school. Since most students are found in some form of junior-senior high school, this level of teaching will be examined first. A consideration of teaching in the senior high school will follow.

THE JUNIOR HIGH SCHOOL

The junior high school was designed as an institution to ease the transition from the elementary school to the high school and from childhood to adolescence. In order to comprehend what it is like to be a junior high teacher, one must understand the changes that take place in the school and the child during this period.

Transition from Elementary to High School

When there is no junior high school, the child goes from the self-contained classroom of the elementary school to the departmental organization of the high school. This is a marked change for the student. He goes from the security of one elementary teacher, who knew him well as an individual, to the initially confusing experience of having five or six different teachers in the high school. Now he is one of perhaps 150 students a single high school teacher may have; before, he was one of 25 or 30 in his elementary class. He knew his classmates well in the elementary school. In the high school he must adjust to many new classmates.

The elementary school is generally considered to be child centered, i.e., we focus our attention on the child and attempt to meet his individual needs. On the other hand, the high school is subject centered. The child goes from a situation in which he was the prime concern to a situation in which the subject matter perhaps becomes more important.

Another change that takes place in going from elementary school to high school is the shift from a group pattern to an individual pattern. Formerly, all studied the same subjects and engaged in similar activities. Now, programs are individualized. One does not necessarily study the same things as his friends.

Then, there are the differences in evaluation between the elementary and the high school. The youngster may be exposed to change from ability marking to achievement marking. Whereas his marks were based largely upon his capacity as an individual (ability marking), he may now be graded to a great extent on how he compares to the group (achievement marking).

Finally, there may be a change in class grouping practices. Many elementary schools make use of heterogeneous grouping—students representing a wide range of abilities are found in the same classroom. High schools, however, frequently utilize some form of homogeneous grouping—students are grouped by some special criterion or criteria, for example, IQ, school marks, and teacher opinion.

Transition from Childhood to Early Adolescence

In going from childhood to early adolescence, the transition of the junior high school years, a number of adjustments must be made. Perhaps the most apparent change that takes place is the physical one. Some youngsters get their growth spurt early, others later. Look at any eighth grade class and you will be struck by the physical differences among the children. Several of the girls could pass for sixteen or seventeen; others appear to be fifth graders. There may be as much as a difference of one foot in the height of the boys. All this change requires an adjustment to the new physical self: an adjustment that is difficult and painful for many youngsters.

The peer group (age mates) becomes important. What they do, what they think, and what they wear becomes dominant in the life of the early adolescent. It is an age of fads, of conforming to the group. At the same time there is an early striving for some independence and rebellion against adult authority. The youngsters begin to be quite critical of adults.

The tendency to accept the standards of the peer group frequently brings on a clash with parents. Up to this point the youngster's values have been mostly those of his parents. Now he begins to question their values and search for his own. Thus, there is a moral adjustment to be made. The right and wrong of things becomes a problem.

This period may also be a time of questioning the validity of religious beliefs. A conflict may present itself due to the possibility of confusing emotional feelings and religious belief. For some it may be a time of religious awakening. At any rate, the area of religion is often a sensitive point for this age group.

There is also the adjustment to sex, a topic of much interest to the junior high school youngster. There are problems and concerns about getting along with the other sex. This interest comes earlier for the girls, about seventh grade. The boys discover girls about grade 8. In both cases, however, there is quite a range of individual differences. This new interest in the opposite sex surely adds another dimension to school.

These adjustments make for a certain amount of instability. Students can act quite adult at one minute and quite childish the next. Their mood swings tend to be extreme. They are frequently sensitive, feel awkward, frustrated, and dissatisfied. There is a certain amount of insecurity and anxiety. For some these are enjoyable years; for many they are confusing times. Superimposed on all this is the need for acceptance and the need to be understood.

Special Functions of the Junior High School

With some understanding of the changes that take place in the school and the child in the transition from elementary to high school and from childhood to early adolescence, we can approach the special functions of the junior high school. Effective teaching in the junior high school depends upon a clear understanding of the institution's functions: integration, exploration, guidance, differentiation, socialization, and articulation.[4]

Integration in the junior high school has to do with the bringing together of the past learnings and skills the student has acquired and the fusing of content into a whole. A broad general education should be provided and the basic common skills should be further developed. The use of a block of time (two or more periods in length in which two or more subjects are taught together) is a great aid to integration. Often, for instance, English and social studies are taught in a block of time. The purpose of the integration can be defeated, however, if each subject is taught separately, which too frequently is the case.

The opportunity for *exploration* should be offered to students. They should be able to probe their interests, aptitudes, and abilities in order to make future educational and vocational plans and to come to know themselves better. Such explorations should help them to develop a wide range of interests, grow in self-knowledge, and learn more about the world of work. This exploratory approach, of course, should carry over into the classroom. A type of learning that enables students to discover things for themselves can be particularly effective in junior high school.

Guidance is a most important function. These youngsters need help in making adjustments, getting the most out of their present educational experience, and making future educational and vocational plans. Guidance, however, does not consist of telling students what to do; good guidance is helping other people solve their own problems. Not all guidance is to be done by the guidance staff, for the teacher will be involved in assisting students. Extended homeroom periods can be used for group guidance in which the problems and concerns common to the class can be taken up.

Differentiation has to do with providing the opportunities and the facilities so that each youngster may have the chance to real-

<hr/>

[4] William T. Gruhn and Harl B. Douglas, *The Modern Junior High School*. Second edition (New York: The Ronald Press Co., 1956), pp. 31–32.

ize his potential. It means recognizing individual differences and doing something about them; it means offering a diversified program; and it means accepting the fact that not all students will perform at the same level. Each teacher must consider in his planning the different abilities, aptitudes, aspirations, backgrounds, and interests of his students.

The function of *socialization* implies that the school will seek to prepare its students for entry into society. It also implies that the school will assist students in developing and improving their social relations with peers, particularly those of the opposite sex. The school can help to prepare students for entry into society by providing experiences in democratic living. The students can be assisted with their social relations through well-planned activities conducted by the school. It is in the area of boy–girl relationships that the junior high school sometimes comes into conflict with parents. Not all parents are in agreement about how quickly maturation in this area should occur. Social dances on a "date" basis in seventh grade, for example, are deemed inappropriate by some parents. It should not be inferred that dances are the only means of promoting social relations among these youngsters. There are many kinds of informal situations that can be offered by the school for this purpose.

In providing a smooth transition from the elementary to the high school, the junior high fulfills the function of *articulation*. One way in which this can be done is to keep the seventh grade basically self-contained (one teacher teaching the same group of students most of their subjects); to use a block of time in eighth grade; and to have departmentalization in ninth grade. In this manner the change from one teacher to many teachers is not so abrupt. It also helps to assure that at least one teacher will know the student well.

Actually, the junior high school moves the student from a kind of education suited to childhood to a kind of education suited to adolescence. Organization and administration are important, but the effectiveness of the junior high school in carrying out its functions is determined to a great extent by the junior high school teacher.

Teaching in the Junior High School

There is quite a turnover among junior high school teachers. Many of them do not care to teach students of this age group after an initial exposure; they find the youngsters difficult to control and trying to work with. Perhaps a good number of these teachers do not understand the junior high school student. Others who leave want to go "up" to the senior high school and use the junior high as a stepping stone. Frequently teachers, and some administrators too, refer to going "down" to the junior high when speaking of teaching there. They seem to put a stigma on teaching in junior high and status on teaching in senior high.

It does take a particular type of teacher to work effectively at this level of education. He must know and understand these young people. He must *want* to work with them. He needs to have, in a sense, the orientation of the elementary teacher toward his students, yet he needs the depth of knowledge of the high school teacher. Such a teacher is difficult to prepare in a four-year college program. He must be ready to work in a basically self-contained class, a block of time, a core arrangement, or a departmental organization.

Self-contained class. The junior high teacher may be assigned to a self-contained classroom in which he will be required to teach English, social studies, science, and math. Such a situation would more typically be found in a seventh-grade class.[5] This is a challenge that requires quite a range and depth of knowledge in addition to teaching skill.

A wise teacher will make use of his understanding of this age group, regardless of the administrative arrangement under which

[5] Grace S. Wright and Edith S. Greer, *The Junior High School: A Survey of Grades 7-8-9 in Junior and Junior-Senior High Schools 1959–60*, U.S. Office of Education OE-20046 (Washington, D.C.: Government Printing Office, 1963), p. 19.

he may be teaching. These youngsters are active and growing. There seems little sense in continually demanding absolute quiet and motionlessness from them. It is much better to involve them in an active kind of learning in which, to a great extent, they can work on their own. Pupil–teacher planning, through which students help to determine the learning activities, can be quite effective. The use of committees and other small groups is a good technique. These kinds of activities utilize the developing need of junior high youngsters for independence and recognition. Devise projects and assignments that take into account individual differences. Not all students need to be doing the same thing in the same way at the same time. Try also in assignments to capitalize upon the growing criticalness of the students and their interest in exploring and discovering things for themselves.

Block of time. Block-of-time classes are most commonly found in seventh or eighth grade; the most frequent subject combinations are English–social studies or science–math.[6] In this extended period of time, the two subjects are supposed to be taught in an integrated fashion. The purpose is twofold: to provide for integration, a special function of the junior high, and to provide a situation in which at least one teacher can come to know the individual student well. The latter purpose is usually accomplished, for the block teacher has time to know his students well. As was said before, however, integrated teaching does not always take place: often the two subjects are taught separately. One reason for this is that it takes skill and careful planning to weave the two subjects together. Not all teachers have this skill, unfortunately, and some do not care to put the time and effort into the planning required for effective block teaching.

Core. The term *core* has come to have many meanings. The author attended one conference where junior high administrators spent forty-five minutes trying to agree on the meaning of core! Here core is used to mean a teaching situation in which (1) a block of time is used and (2) several subjects are fused in the

---

[6] *Ibid.,* p. 23.

study of problem-centered units which have real meaning for the students.

A good core teacher is a rare item. He must have superior teaching skill and a real command of much knowledge. In teaching a core built around the problem of establishing a model community, for example, many kinds of knowledge and skill can be integrated. The language arts would be employed in reading and in written and oral reports; the area of social studies would be involved in form of government, geography, economy, and so forth; and subjects such as health, science, and math would be considered in various community problems, research, and computations. You can well realize the knowledge and skill such teaching would require.

Departmental.[7] A vast majority of junior high schools are departmentalized by the ninth grade.[8] With such an arrangement, one teacher teaches the same subject to many different boys and girls. He is, or ought to be, a specialist in that subject. It may be that he will teach two courses in the same subject-area, such as algebra and general math, but he is still a math specialist. Perhaps the point made earlier in the chapter—that it is difficult to prepare a good junior high teacher in the conventional four-year college program—is now more obvious to you. It is difficult indeed to develop competency in English, math, science, and social studies, a concentration in one of these subjects, and professional skills, not to mention the necessary general education, in a four-year program.

A typical day. The average junior high teacher has a typical school-day of seven or eight hours, including lunch, with six periods of 55 to 59 minutes in length.[9] He spends about 80 percent of his time in teaching and the balance on out-of-class activities.[10] The out-of-class activities consist of such things as supervising

---

[7] A fuller discussion of departmental teaching will be found in the next section of the chapter, which is on the senior high school.

[8] *Ibid.*, p. 19.

[9] *Ibid.*, p. 78.

[10] *Ibid.*, p. 84.

study halls and the lunchroom and sponsoring clubs or other extraclass activities.

The club program is an important part of the teacher's work. It is through these clubs that a youngster can probe and pursue already-established interests or explore new ones. The kinds of clubs included would evolve from subjects studied (Math Club, Science Club, and so on) or from vocational or avocational interests (Radio Club, Photography Club, and so on). The educational value of these extraclass activities is emphasized in making them a part of the regular school day as many schools have done.

If the junior high school is the place for you to teach, your typical day will be filled with challenge, excitement, and reward in working with these unpredictable, at times frustrating but always interesting, young people.

THE SENIOR HIGH SCHOOL

As a high school teacher you will be part of a unique institution which attempts to serve the needs of all youth: those who will continue their education beyond high school, those who will marry or go into the world of work or the armed forces after graduation, and those who will never graduate. The way in which these three groups of youth are served will vary from high school to high school. A truly comprehensive high school, though, will attempt to meet the needs of all these young people.

A pronounced problem today, however, is that some schools seem to be focusing their attention on the college-bound student, to the detriment of the general program. Some high schools seem to be run for the benefit of the college preparatory student. These students, as important as they may be, do not constitute the major portion of young people in today's high schools. If the 30 percent of the students who drop out before graduation from high school is added to the 35 percent who graduate but do not go further in their education, it can be seen that the majority of students are *not* going on to higher education. Their needs must also be met if the American high school is to fulfill its purpose.

Functions and Purposes of the High School

Here is not the place for a prolonged discussion of the functions and purposes of the high school, but, as a potential secondary teacher, you do need to know something of the "why" of the
institution in which you may work. A number of statements related to the functions and purposes of the high school have been
made.[11] Some of these statements represent marked disagreement
about what the secondary school should be and do. It is the author's view that the following statement of the principal functions
of the secondary school is a good one:

1. To provide schooling for all youth that will enable each person to
   attain the fullest possible development of his potentialities in socially approved ways.
2. To assist each pupil in identifying his potentialities, talents, and
   capabilities.
3. To conserve and transmit knowledge.
4. To inculcate the beliefs, values, traditions, and aspirations of the
   social group.
5. To help the young live more effectively the good life, as envi-
   sioned by the American people.[12]

If the above statement of functions is accepted as a valid one,
then the primary purposes of the secondary school may be stated
as follows:

Self understanding: Provide the opportunities for each pupil
    a. To determine his own talents, potentialities, capacities and en-
       during interests.

---

[11] See, for example, Commission on the Reorganization of the Secondary
School, *Cardinal Principles of Secondary Education,* U.S. Office of Education Bulletin 1918, No. 35 (Washington, D.C.: Government Printing Office,
1918); Educational Policies Commission, National Education Association,
The Purposes of Education in American Democracy (Washington, D.C.:
the Association, 1938); and Educational Policies Commission, National Education Association, *The Central Purpose of American Education,* (Washington, D.C.: the Association, 1961).
[12] J. Galen Saylor, "Secondary Education," Van Cleve Morris and others,
Becoming an Educator (Boston: Houghton Mifflin in Company, 1963), p. 222.

b. To formulate proper aspiration levels and a valid set of personal expectations and career motivations.

Individual development: Provide the educational experiences that will enable each pupil

a. To develop his intellectual powers to the fullest.

b. To acquire the basic knowledge, concepts, and understandings in the major fields of study that contribute to maximum self-realization.

c. To develop to the maximum extent possible his unique talents and capabilities in a socially approved manner.

Vocational orientation: Provide opportunities for each pupil

a. To determine his interest in and capabilities for scholarly study of a specialized field of knowledge.

b. To explore his interest in appropriate occupational fields, and for those who have determined, with the aid of counsel, that they do not wish to pursue formal study in scholarly fields of endeavor beyond high school, to participate in appropriate pre-vocational and vocational educational activities.

Civic responsibility: Help each pupil

To develop attitudes of civil, social and political responsibility, to acquire the knowledge, understandings, and abilities necessary in the exercise of wise citizenship, and to act in conformity with democratic ideals.[13]

The High School Student

The high school student continues with the adjustments begun in early adolescence and adds others as he progresses through this period. The developmental tasks[14] identified by Robert J. Havighurst for adolescence are:

1. Achieving new and more mature relations with one's age mates of both sexes.

2. Achieving a masculine or feminine social role.

[13] *Ibid.,* p. 226.
[14] Those tasks, as defined in Chapter 3, that are to be accomplished during a particular period of development. If they are not accomplished at that time they delay further development and become more difficult to complete at a later time.

3. Accepting one's physique and using the body effectively.
4. Achieving emotional independence of parents and other adults.
5. Achieving assurance of economic independence.
6. Selecting and preparing for a vocation.
7. Preparing for marriage and family life.
8. Developing intellectual skills and concepts necessary for civic competence.
9. Desiring and achieving socially responsible behavior.
10. Acquiring a set of values and an ethical system as a guide to behavior.[15]

The attempt of the adolescent to accomplish these tasks has direct implications for the school in general and for the teacher in particular. Such tasks as selecting and preparing for a vocation, achieving socially responsible behavior, and acquiring a set of values are of concern to the school. The teacher surely is affected by the tasks dealing with values, behavior, and the achievement of independence, for these directly influence the way he will work with his students and the kind of relationship he will have with them.

Teaching the High School Student

As a high school teacher you will probably have the responsibility for teaching five classes daily, supervising a study hall, and sponsoring some student activity. Usually you are afforded one free period a day for planning or other work. These activities will constitute your work each day. The following aspects of that work will be discussed: discipline, planning, teaching, and working with students.

Discipline. Discipline is considered first because it is frequently the most difficult problem for beginning teachers. A solution cannot be given for each and every discipline problem you will face, but some general guidelines may be of help to you.

First, *many discipline problems are really teaching problems.*

[15] Robert J. Havighurst, *Human Development and Education* (New York: Longmans, Green & Co., 1953), pp. 111–158.

If you can get and keep your class interested and if you can provide an active kind of learning for your students, you will have automatically eliminated many behavior problems. An interested and active class is usually a well-behaved one. Furthermore, through wise planning you can anticipate some of the things that may present problems and provide for them.

Second, *you generally get from students what you expect of them.* It is up to you to set standards for students, to point out to them what you expect in the way of classroom behavior. Your class will feel more secure in knowing what you expect. They need and want to know. In most cases, if your standards are fair and reasonable, students will comply with them. *Fair* and *reasonable* are the key words.

Third, *the kind of relationship you establish with students is most important.* If you are prepared to treat them as adults, if you are sincere, and if you respect them as individuals, they usually will cooperate with you. Realize, of course, that as a teacher you cannot be "one of them" again. How you relate to your students will largely be a function of your particular personality, but you will run into difficulty if you are too friendly. Certainly you should not be aloof. Too much familiarity, however, frequently presents problems.

Fourth, *be consistent.* Do not have wide temperament swings from being a "good guy" to being a "tyrant." Try to present an even disposition to the class. Be consistent also in the way you react to behavior. What was acceptable yesterday should not become unacceptable today. What was fair for one student yesterday should also be fair for another student today.

Fifth, *do not make threats you cannot carry out.* To say that you are "going to fail the whole class," for example, is an empty threat that they know you will not carry out. Actually, punishing the whole class for the misbehavior of one student whose identity you cannot determine is a poor practice. It surely does not help the morale of the class nor your relationship with them.

Sixth, *try to understand the student's behavior.* In spite of all you do, there will still be some problems of control. Try not to focus on the "what" of the misbehavior but on the "why" of it. Why did the student behave as he did? Many times, for example, misbehavior is a means of gaining attention and recognition. If this is the case, try to find some fruitful way in which the student may gain the attention and recognition he desires. Praise and a successful experience for a student can work wonders.

Seventh, *settle your own discipline problems.* Endeavor, as much as is possible, to solve your own discipline problems. These are your problems and you, not someone else, should solve them. Do not constantly send students to the principal's office. He will begin to doubt your competence and so will the students. Occasionally you may have to take a discipline problem beyond your classroom, but this should be the exception, not the rule.

Last, remember that *the purpose of disciplinary action is to change behavior, not to seek revenge.* Your purpose is not to "get even" with the student; you want him to change what he has been doing. Above all, if you feel that you must give some punishment, do not give school work as that punishment. It is difficult enough to get some students interested in school. Do not make the situation worse by associating school work with punishment.

Planning. Planning is absolutely necessary for effective teaching. In the beginning, much of this planning will have to be written out in detailed form. Later, you will not necessarily have to write out long plans. As you gain experience and skill, you can think through what you want to do and put it down briefly. The important point is that you *must* plan.

You will need to do both short-range and long-range planning. Of course you will need to know what you are doing each day and why, but you need to have overall plans. You need to have in mind what you are going to accomplish this marking period, this term, and this year.

At the start, it is hard to plan, for you do not know the length of time it takes to teach a particular topic. Notice that the word *teach* was used and not *cover* a particular topic. You may "cover" the material, but there is no assurance that the student has learned it. Timing and pacing come with experience. There are, however, materials available to assist you in your initial planning, such as courses of study or syllabi.

In your planning, consider the interests and needs of your students. In view of their concern for managing their own affairs, let them share in at least part of the planning. If they have been unaccustomed to this responsibility, it may take you some time to bring them up to this level. It will be worth the time, and it will add much to your class.

Plan to use a variety of methods and materials. Do not fall into the rut of continually doing things in the same way. There has been enough of "read the chapter, answer the questions at the end of the chapter, and fill in your workbooks." Devise different ways of presenting an idea, for in secondary teaching you will need to present the same idea in various ways to be certain that it is understood. Make use of audio-visual aids, but do not overdo it. (One class the author knew of was called "The Early Show" by the students because of the number of films used.) And, as you gain experience, do not be afraid to try something new.

Teaching. As a high school teacher, you will be assigned to a department and will work under your department head. Since you will be a junior member of the department, your teaching assignment may be less desirable, that is, you may be given classes that tend to be larger in size and subjects that are not as sought after by senior members of the department—those subjects that tend to enroll students of lower academic ability who may present more discipline problems. It is indeed wise to find out what your teaching assignment will be, as well as what kind of school and community this is in which to live and work, before you sign your contract with the school district. Actually, it would be better to assign the new teacher a lighter load so that his many first-year adjustments would be made easier.

Ordinarily, you can expect to have one, two, or even three separate preparations. For example, you may be assigned to teach five classes of first-year algebra—one preparation; you may be given three classes of first-year algebra and two classes of plane geometry—two preparations. It is to be hoped that the beginning teacher would be given no more than two preparations, though more difficult programs are commonly assigned.

One problem you will soon notice about teaching several classes of the same subject is the difficulty of keeping track of just where you are and what you are doing in each class. You will find that it pays to keep separate plans for each class on which you note just what was accomplished each day. This will help to prevent you from presenting the same lesson twice to the same class. (It has been done!) Furthermore, it should help to eliminate having to ask your class, "Where were we?" or, "Did we cover this?" You are the teacher; you should know.

Repeating the same lesson three or more times a day can surely take the edge of freshness from your presentation. True, the students in each class are different, but the material is basically the same. You really have to keep your enthusiasm up the third or fourth time around. One good solution is to run each class differently, if the course of study can be so handled. It may not be a good idea to attempt this in your first year, however, because it is easier to run the classes in a similar fashion.

If you have planned well, you should be using a variety of methods and materials in your teaching. Do not rely solely on the textbook as a source of material. There are other more current and varied materials that may also be used—newspapers and current periodicals, for example. These make your courses more timely and real for your students. Furthermore, deliberately planning to use a variety of methods helps to prevent you from falling into the habit of using but one method, something that is all too easy to do.

The size of your student load will have its effect upon your teaching. Dr. Conant recommended, for instance, that English teachers have no more than 100 students[16] so that they would be

---

[16] James B. Conant, *The American High School Today* (New York: McGraw-Hill Book Company, 1959), p. 51.

able to assign and correct a theme a week from each student. A reasonable amount of work should be expected of students, but you must be careful not to assign more work than you can sensibly handle. Remember that you do have to allow yourself time for rest and relaxation too.

Working with students. You will have many contacts with students outside your classroom. There will be certain supervisory duties to perform, sponsoring of clubs and activities, guiding students, and, in general, participating in the life of the school.

The supervisory responsibilities may consist of study hall, lunchroom, or hall duty. Such duties tend to place you in the role of "policeman" and are not viewed favorably by many teachers. There is also doubt about the value of many a study hall for the student. To cram several hundred students into the auditorium for a study period does not provide optimum conditions for concentrated study. All we can say is that you should make the best of your supervisory assignments and endeavor not to let this aspect of your work discourage you or deteriorate your relations with students.

If your relationship with students is good, they may come to you for advice on a number of things. It may be that they simply want to talk over a problem with you. As a young teacher, you will have the advantage of being close to them in age. Your closeness in age to the adolescent period may attract more students to you. We cannot predict what problems young people will bring to you, but some of these problems may go beyond your role as teacher. In such cases, it is better to refer the student to those more able and qualified to help than you are.

SOME RECENT DEVELOPMENTS
IN SECONDARY EDUCATION

The secondary school is changing, though not so rapidly as the elementary school. Change is taking place in organization, curriculum and instruction, methods and techniques, materials, and devices for teaching and learning. Much of this change will be discussed in Chapter 7 under "Educational Innovations." Here, attention will be given to illustrative curriculum changes and to Dr. Conant's latest report on the comprehensive high school.[17]

Illustrative Curriculum Changes

The secondary school curriculum has been the subject of much study in the last decade. The shift in emphasis after the first Sputnik in 1957 toward the academic side of the curriculum focused on the fields of science and mathematics, and it is in these two fields that most work has been done. A brief examination of the developments in science and mathematics as well as social studies will illustrate recent and continuing activity in the secondary school curriculum.

In science, study of the curriculum has generally proceeded in the separate teaching fields (biology, physics, chemistry, and so forth) rather than in the field of science as a whole. An attempt has been made to move from descriptive science with the emphasis on facts, to an inquiry or discovery approach emphasizing understanding. Most of the curriculum projects have been supported by the National Science Foundation. Some of these projects are:

Biological Sciences Curriculum Study (BSCS)
Physical Science Study Committee (PSSC)
The Chemical Education Materials Study (CHEM Study)
Junior High School Science Project
The Science Curriculum: K-12 Approach

Research scientists and science educators have worked together to replace an outdated body of knowledge with truly current knowledge and approaches. As one speaks with science teachers, however, one finds that not all are enthusiastic over the "new science." Some feel that certain materials and approaches, those of

[17] James B. Conant, *The Comprehensive High School: A Second Report to Interested Citizens* (New York: McGraw-Hill Book Company, 1967).

the BSCS for example, are perhaps too difficult for many high school students.

In the field of mathematics similar study has taken place. Here, however, studies have tended to concentrate more on the unified field of mathematics rather than on its separate teaching areas. Much has been said and written about the "new math." What are the characteristics of the new mathematics?

1. It eliminates those topics that are relatively unimportant.
2. It integrates those topics that are important.
3. It introduces recent and important developments in mathematics.
4. It emphasizes the structure of mathematics, rather than isolated topics.
5. It introduces subject matter to students earlier than was previously thought possible.[18]

Certainly the emphasis on the structure of mathematics is a marked improvement. Too often in the past no relationship between algebra and geometry was evident, for example. And the offering of such subjects as calculus at the secondary level has been of particular value to those pursuing the collegiate study of science, engineering, or mathematics.

In mathematics, as in science, the discovery approach has been used in an attempt to emphasize understanding of rather than simply performance of a function or a process. And, again, the National Science Foundation has given the most support to the various curriculum projects, a sampling of which would include the following:

The School Mathematics Study Group (SMSG)
The University of Illinois Committee on School Mathematics (UICSM)
Syracuse University–Webster College Madison Project
The University of Maryland Mathematics Project

[18] Allen F. Strehler, "What's New About the New Math?" *Saturday Review,* March 21, 1964, pp. 69, 84.

Geometry Project of the Department of Mathematics of Stanford University.

Some attention has been given to the social studies, but no dramatic curriculum reorganization has occurred comparable to that
in science and mathematics. "Project Social Studies" of the United
States Office of Education seems to offer some promise. Funds
have been made available for nine curriculum centers at major
universities and for numerous research projects and developmental activities. The curriculum centers attempt to do one or more
of the following:

> (1) To redefine the aims of social studies curriculum at one or more
> grade levels; (2) to develop sequences of presenting subject matter
> that are based on what is known about human development and the
> teaching-learning processes; (3) to work out methods and prepare
> materials to meet specific needs; (4) to try out new methods and
> materials and evaluate them; and (5) to disseminate information
> about the most promising methods and materials.[19]

The inclusion of the social studies in the 1964 Amendments to the
National Defense Education Act afforded stimulus to further curriculum reform.

There are some differences of opinion about the kinds of
changes that should occur in social studies. For example, Jerome
Bruner of Harvard University, who is developing a social studies
curriculum for Educational Service Incorporated, is attempting to
identify basic organizing principles in the social studies. He is focusing on the behavior of man in society—what is human about
human beings, how they got that way, and how they can be made
more human. On the other hand, Dr. Mark M. Krug, professor of
education in history at the University of Chicago, objects to Bruner's approach. He believes that Bruner would place too much
emphasis on the behavioral sciences; that attempting to find
meaningful patterns in history is impossible, and that such a cur-

[19] Gerald R. Smith, "Project Social Studies—A Report," *School Life,* 45:
25, July, 1963.

riculum would discourage able young people from becoming history teachers.[20]

The Second Conant Report

Dr. Conant, in *The Comprehensive High School: A Second Report to Interested Citizens,* presented the findings of his follow-up study on the American high school. In general, he found that there had been significant improvement with reference to his original twenty-one recommendations contained in *The American High School Today.* Only 10 percent of the sample of 2,000 schools,[21] however, met all of his requirements. Furthermore, he singled out the "chaotic" state of financing of education as being responsible for much of the inequality of educational opportunity.

He found that most schools had so organized their day that a student could take five academic subjects plus art or music and physical education, and that most schools now offer four years of one modern foreign language. He also found that almost all schools offered the following: courses in business education, home economics, music, and art; courses for slow learners; ability grouping in one or more academic subjects; and summer school. The new physics, chemistry, or biology was offered by about 65 percent of the schools, and calculus was given by 40 percent of the schools in the sample.[22]

However, he still found the ratio of guidance counselors to students to be unsatisfactory. Only about 32 percent of the sample had a ratio of 1 counselor to 349 or less students. (Conant had originally recommended a ratio of 1 counselor to 250 to 300 students.) Courses in the Advanced Placement Program were available in only about 30 percent of the schools. In the case of the

---

[20] Donald S. Rosser, Contributing Editor, "Curriculum Frontiers: Agonizing Reappraisal," *NJEA Review,* 40:12, March, 1967.

[21] The schools selected for study were medium-sized (enrollment between 750 and 2,000 students) comprehensive high schools.

[22] James B. Conant, *The Comprehensive High School: A Second Report to Interested Citizens* (New York: McGraw-Hill Book Company, 1967), pp. 66–67.

ratio of English teachers to their students, Dr. Conant indicated that only about 26 percent of the sample had a ratio of 1 to 120 or less.[23]

Dr. Conant was most concerned about finding that only slightly more than half of the medium-sized widely comprehensive high schools surveyed were adequately staffed. This is based upon the Educational Policies Commission's recommendation of a ratio of certified professional staff to students of 1 to 20. Actually, he believes that to be really adequate in a number of respects a school should have a ratio of 1 to 17.4 or less, and he suggests that the certified professional staff–student ratio can be used as a first approximation to a judgment of the adequacy of the offerings of the type of school studied.[24]

The inadequate way in which our schools are financed, then, accounts for the inequality of educational opportunity; it is in this area that something must be done. Dr. Conant believes that new methods of financing public education must be developed.[25]

SUGGESTED ACTIVITIES

1. Interview a junior high school teacher and a senior high school teacher about their work in secondary education. Attempt to determine differences and similarities in their attitudes toward their students and the subjects they teach.
2. Form a committee to plan a debate on the junior high school type of organization as compared to the newer idea of the middle school discussed in Chapter 3.
3. Select a high school subject of special interest to you and consult the professional literature to find out about new developments in that field. Prepare a report of your findings.
4. Discuss the advantages and the disadvantages of the comprehensive high school serving all students as compared with specialized high

[23] *Ibid.*
[24] *Ibid.*, pp. 14–16.
[25] *Ibid.*, p. 80. The problem of financing public education will be discussed in Chapter 6, "The American Public School System."

schools for the academically able, for the vocational student, or for other special groups of students.

5. Make arrangements, with your instructor's approval, for a high school principal to speak to the class on significant changes in secondary education in the last decade.
6. Form a committee to plan and prepare a panel discussion on the problem of the high school dropout.
7. Investigate the availability and quality, as best you can determine, of private and parochial education at the secondary level in your state.
8. Plan with your instructor to visit a high school in your area that is experimenting with new methods and materials in secondary education.
9. Discuss the role of the guidance department in the secondary school. How effective was the guidance program in your high school?

SELECTED REFERENCES

Alberty, Harold B., and Alberty, Elsie J. *Reorganizing the High School Curriculum.* Third edition. New York: The Macmillan Company, 1963. A practical text that provides an analysis of today's high school. Conflicts and issues of secondary education are dealt with.

Association for Supervision and Curriculum Development. *The Junior High School We Need.* Washington, D.C.: National Education Association, 1961. Characteristics of early adolescents having educational implications are identified. Suggests criteria for junior high school programs and proposes needed changes to meet current demands.

Alexander, William M. *The Changing Secondary School Curriculum: Readings.* New York: Holt, Rinehart and Winston, 1967. A collection of opinions and theories about complex and controversial curriculum issues. Attention is given to the changing secondary school curriculum.

Benjamen, Harold. *The Saber-Tooth Curriculum.* New York: McGraw-Hill Book Company, 1939. A satire illustrating the resistance to curriculum change.

Bossing, Nelson L., and Cramer, Roscoe V. *The Junior High School.*

Boston: Houghton Mifflin Company, 1965. A general reference on the junior high school. Considers such topics as development, curriculum and instruction, student personnel administration, and staff and facilities.

Brown, B. Frank. *The Nongraded High School.* Englewood Cliffs, N.J.: Prentice-Hall, 1963. Presents a new approach being taken to secondary education in Melbourne, Florida.

Clark, Leonard H., Klein, Raymond L., and Burks, John B. *The American Secondary School Curriculum.* New York: The Macmillan Company, 1965. A clear overview of the foundations of the high school curriculum in the U.S. and abroad, with special reference to current trends. Abundant bibliographical references.

Conant, James B. *The American High School Today.* New York: McGraw-Hill Book Company, 1959. A well-known study with recommendations for improvement of the high school.

Conant, James B. *The Comprehensive High School: A Second Report to Interested Citizens.* New York: McGraw-Hill Book Company, 1967. A follow up of his earlier study of the American high school. Points up significant improvement with still much to be done, particularly in the area of school finance.

Davis, E. Dale. *Focus on Secondary Education: An Introduction to Principles and Practices.* Glenview, Ill.: Scott, Foresman and Company, 1966. Covers many aspects of the secondary school, including the role of the teacher and problems and progress in secondary education.

French, William M. *American Secondary Education.* Second edition. New York: The Odyssey Press, 1967. A text on the history, characteristics, and problems of secondary education.

Mallery, David. *High School Students Speak Out.* New York: Harper & Row Publishers, 1962. High school from the students' point of view—what is taught, how it is taught, and how it is run.

National Association of Secondary School Principals. *Instructional Procedures in the Secondary School.* Washington, D.C.: National Education Association, 1962. Thorough study of instructional procedures and practices in the high school.

Trump, J. Lloyd. *Images of the Future.* Urbana, Ill.: Commission on the Experimental Study of the Staff in Secondary Schools, 1959. Some new ideas on the utilization of staff and the organization and program of the secondary school.

VanTil, William, Vars, Gordon F., and Lounsbury, John H. *Modern Education for the Junior High School Years*. Second edition. Indianapolis, Ind.: The Bobbs Merrill Company, 1967. Considers the developments of the junior high school, its foundations, curricular patterns, and methods of teaching.

5   Teaching at the College Level

American higher education is not easily characterized because of its diversity. Certain facts and statistics, however, can be set forth. There are some 500,000 professors teaching about 6,000,000 students in over 2,200 colleges.[1] Most students now attend publicly supported colleges, though most colleges are private.[2] There are a good many small colleges, but a relatively few large institutions enroll a sizable proportion of college students. The rapidly growing junior or community colleges presently constitute close to one third of all institutions of higher learning and account for one out of four students. It has even been predicted that the number of junior colleges will exceed the number of four-year colleges by 1970.

Types of Colleges

The above statements do not really begin to describe the types of colleges in this country. Added to whether the college is large or small, public or private, could be such factors as whether the institution is two years or four years in length; secular or sectarian; primarily resident or nonresident; urban or rural; for one sex or coeducational; highly selective in its admissions policies or not; or accredited or nonaccredited. And this list is not complete. In

[1] U.S. Office of Education, *Education Directory, 1965–1966: Part 3, Higher Education*, FS 5,250:50000–66/Part 111 (Washington, D.C.: Government Printing Office, 1966), p. 10.
[2] *Ibid.*, p. 11.

other words, it is very difficult to classify the many kinds of colleges there are. We can, however, set up some rough groupings for our purposes here.

1. *Two year colleges.* These may be junior colleges, community colleges, or technical institutes, but they do not offer the third or fourth year of college. More will be said of the community college later in the chapter.
2. *Liberal arts colleges.* These institutions offer liberal education, preprofessional education, and some specialization. They are predominantly private and frequently small in size.
3. *Multi-purpose colleges.* A number of state colleges, formerly teachers colleges, are in this category. This type of college offers, in addition to general or liberal education, a variety or programs such as teacher education, business administration, and nursing education.
4. *Universities.* Several schools or colleges are a feature of the university, as is research. The great public and private universities are found in this category, which accounts for about one half of the enrollment in higher education. Of course, every institution that calls itself a "university" may not truly be a university in the full sense of the term.
5. *Professional schools.* These colleges provide education in a special area such as medicine, engineering, teaching, and other professional and technical fields. They have been established to meet career needs. There has, however, been a trend to provide most professional education at the graduate level.
6. *Graduate schools.* Work beyond the bachelor's degree is offered by graduate schools. Students matriculate for master's degrees, doctor's degrees, and possibly postdoctoral study. Graduate schools are enjoying a fast rate of growth. For example, during the academic year ending June, 1965, approximately 129,000 graduate degrees were earned, according to the U.S. Office of Education. This represented an 11 percent increase in master's degrees and a 14 percent increase in doctor's degrees over the previous academic year.

7. *Others.* This last category is added because some institutions do not fit into any of the above groupings. It includes such institutions as military colleges, "experimental" colleges, and other types not included above.

Today's College Student

College students today are better prepared and more serious than students before them. DeYoung and Wynn have said:

> The new generation of college students appears to be more skeptical of easy answers, more constructively critical of the American social scene, more academically responsible, and even more idealistic than other recent generations. Their enthusiastic and effective response to the Peace Corps, one of the greatest idealistic challenges to any generation of college students, must give pause to the critics who proclaimed them a lost, soft generation without purpose or morality.[3]

Most of today's students work to earn part of their college expenses, and a good proportion earn more than half of these expenses. A goodly number are married, something that was quite unusual years ago.

From the standpoint of race and religion, student bodies are more representative than they used to be. Some institutions, however, still have a way to go in the matter of discrimination on the basis of race and religion. It is also true that more and more students are coming from "working-class" families, so that we have a better distribution based upon socio-economic status.

Of ten students who begin at a particular college, probably only four or five will remain to be graduated. Perhaps another one or two of the ten students will transfer and be graduated from another institution. It is unfortunate that nearly half the students will drop out, but what is more unfortunate is that many of them will be very able students. This represents quite a loss to our society. Perhaps part of the problem is that we do not suffi-

[3] Chris A. DeYoung and Richard Wynn, *American Education,* Fifth edition (New York: McGraw-Hill Book Company, 1964), p. 212.

ciently challenge our students. Anyone who has worked with college freshmen over a period of years knows with what eagerness a good many of them come. They are fresh; they are new. Their expectations for college are frequently high, though sometimes unrealistic. We also know, however, that many come for less than the acquisition of erudition. According to a survey conducted by the Educational Testing Service in 1964, which involved 13,000 students entering 23 colleges, slightly more than half [50.8 percent] of the students indicated that their major interest in college was "social life." Only 18.5 precent said that pursuit of ideas and the cultivation of the intellect was their chief interest.

Purposes of Higher Education

Space does not permit a lengthy discussion of the purposes of higher education, though we do want to say a word about them before going on to the main section of this chapter, *the work of the college teacher.*

Certainly there are many purposes for higher educaton. One need only consult the statement of purposes in a number of college catalogues to see this. One difficulty, however, is that the purposes of the institution may not be the same as those of the faculty or the students. If the purposes of all three groups were detailed, the list would indeed be a long one.

Perhaps we can simplify our consideration of purposes by stating that among the generally accepted purposes of higher education would be found the following:

To provide opportunity for individual development of able people.
To transmit the cultural heritage.
To add to existing knowledge through research and creative ability.
To help translate learning into equipment for living and for social advance.
To serve the public interest directly.[4]

[4] Educational Policies Commission, *Higher Education in a Decade of Decision* (Washington, D.C.: National Education Association, 1957), pp. 6–10.

THE WORK OF THE COLLEGE TEACHER

The work of the college teacher consists of teaching, research and writing, working with students, academic service, professional activities, and a category we have designated as "other activities." Each of these will be examined in turn.

Teaching

As Logan Wilson has said, in speaking of priorities in higher education, "Our primary obligation to students in residence implies a top priority for the teaching function."[5] Teaching is indeed the most important part of the professor's work. Yet, "compared to the prestige and recognition, monetary as well as intangible, attaching to scholarly attainment, the few awards for distinguished teaching are pathetic."[6] Because of the rewards afforded by some institutions for research and publication, many faculty members do come to feel that teaching is of secondary importance. Therefore, they do not put forth the time and effort necessary for effective teaching. They forget the basic responsibility they have to teach and to teach well. Mark Van Doren has observed that "the words of a teacher bear so many responsibilities that if all of them were present in his mind together he would grow as silent as the grave."[7]

Entry into college teaching. The doctorate is a major pathway to college teaching, though many graduate students come with only the master's degree. Some college teachers come from secondary school teaching, and some come from outside fields such as

[5] Logan Wilson, "Setting Institutional Priorities," Association for Higher Education, *Current Issues in Higher Education, 1965: Pressures and Priorities in Higher Education* (Washington, D.C.: Association for Higher Education, National Education Association, 1965), p. 38. Hereafter cited as *Current Issues, 1965.*

[6] Robert H. Knapp, "The Changing Functions of the College Professor," Nevitt Sanford, ed., *The American College* (New York: John Wiley & Sons, 1963), p. 298.

[7] Mark Van Doren, "The Good Teacher," Herman A. Estrin and Delmer M. Goode, eds., *College and University Teaching* (Dubuque, Iowa: Wm. C. Brown Company, Publishers, 1964), p. 39.

business or the armed services. We will focus our attention on those who come from the graduate schools.

Few Ph.D. programs provide for the development of teaching skill. The emphasis is on research and scholarship. A graduate student may be introduced to college teaching through the teaching assistantship, a dubious device for developing good college teachers. Ralph Morrow said of teaching assistantships:

> In practice they penalize the studies of a student if he is serious about his teaching and penalize his teaching if he is serious about his studies. Consequently, he is put in the pickle of choosing between victimizing himself and victimizing the freshmen he teaches. The graduate student is likely to learn early that to slight teaching is the price of academic survival. The quality of graduate education and novice teachers would be improved if, instead of being supported by being paid to teach, they were paid to educate themselves and given training in teaching as part of that education.[8]

Perhaps a better approach, which Wilbur Miller discussed, is the teaching internship that could be provided by graduate departments:

> In spite of all the disagreements that have arisen regarding the best ways of preparing teachers for our elementary and secondary school systems, one important part of the training seems to have almost universal acceptance. This is the need for some sort of practice teaching or internship where the student spends some time in the classroom under the supervision of an experienced teacher. Isn't it rather strange then that this important area of preparation is almost completely neglected when the education of college teachers is considered? It seems that we have operated under the assumption that the earning of a graduate degree somehow mysteriously qualifies the student to become an expert teacher in the discipline where his graduate work was performed. Even many of the students seem to

[8] Ralph Morrow, "Preparation and Internship of College Teachers," Association for Higher Education, *Current Issues in Higher Education, 1964: Undergraduate Education* (Washington, D.C.: Association for Higher Education, National Education Association, 1964), p. 120. Hereafter cited as *Current Issues, 1964.*

think that the graduate degree brings with it these expert teacher qualifications.[9]

Since the degree does not bring with it "expert teacher qualifications," and since most graduate schools do not provide adequate preparation in teaching for future professors, we will continue to get more than our share of poor teachers in the colleges. Inadequate orientation procedures and less-than-satisfactory guidance frequently provided at staff meetings for the beginning college teacher do little to improve the situation.

Two other factors that compound the poor preparation of many professors are the tradition of "amateurism" in college teaching and the lack of adequate supervision and assistance for the new instructor:

> Another factor which is illuminated by the difficulty even a conscientious neophyte has in learning the techniques of instruction is the strong tradition of "amateurism" in college teaching. As a group, college teachers have been loftily contemptuous of any formal instruction in curriculum design, testing techniques, and formal classroom procedure. . . . Moreover, in the process of learning by doing, when college teachers set out to teach with nothing before them but the remembered model of their own instructors, they are more often than not immune to any except self-criticism. Their undergraduate students, conscious of grades, and unwilling to offend those with such power over them, incline not to protest directly if the teacher is dull, inchoate, or otherwise ineffectual. Professional taboos, together with their own heavy workloads, generally keep deans, chairmen, and even experienced colleagues out of the classroom of the neophyte instructor.[10]

This disdain for preparation in teaching and the professional taboos about visiting the classroom of the beginning instructor have helped to preserve the tradition of "amateurism" in college teaching.

[9] Wilbur C. Miller, "Internship in College Teaching," *Current Issues, 1964,* p. 116.
[10] Bruce Dearing, "Pressures Jeopardizing Quality of Undergraduate Teaching," *Current Issues, 1965,* p. 116.

In summing up our discussion, we do not want to leave the impression that all poor college teaching is due to lack of preparation or emphasis on research and writing:

> Some instructors are not effective teachers because they basically are not effective people. They do not think broadly and logically. They make little effort to establish effective interpersonal relationships. They believe that profound though often disordered thinking in their own reflections, and on advanced themes, excuses negligence in handling elementary matters given to students.[11]

Poor interpersonal relationships, disordered thought, and routine matters badly handled do not make for good teaching.

Undergraduate teaching. The major portion of teaching in higher education is done at the undergraduate level. An instructor may typically have a 12-hour load. This means that he has 12 teaching hours per week for a semester. His teaching load may consist of one, two, or more preparations. For example, an English professor may have two classes of freshman composition for six hours of his load and two different three-credit literature courses for the remaining six hours.

While 12 teaching hours per week may not seem to be much work, it truly is. Added to the 12 class hours are many hours for preparation, reading of student papers and assignments, student conferences, committee meetings, professional reading, and scholarly activities. Some colleges still require a 15-hour load for faculty members, but a number of institutions operate on a nine- or six-hour load. Of course, with a six- or nine-hour load a professor is expected to be very active in research and other scholarly pursuits.

As we mentioned in the chapter on secondary education, the more desirable assignments tend to go to the senior or status members of the department. "Desirable" usually means higher level courses of smaller size, rather than large freshman and sophomore classes of an introductory nature. It is unfortunate that this

---

[11] Richard K. Morton, "Preface to Improved Teaching," Estrin and Goode, *op. cit.,* p. 563.

is the situation in many places for many reasons, one of the most important of which is that lower classmen are deprived of some fine teachers.

The characteristics of the effective college teacher are similar to many of those discussed in Chapter 1, and we do not wish to repeat them here. We would, however, like to consider a few that are particularly pertinent for the college teacher, though we must still remember the following:

> Many studies have been made regarding the characteristics of the good teacher. So far there is no unanimity on the elements of good teaching. No qualities seem to be so essential that their absence results in failure or their presence assures success.[12]

We would think that "knowledge of his subject" would be a very important characteristic for the effective college teacher. Earl McGrath has said that

> . . . "knowledge of his subject" means more properly an acquaintance with the key ideas, the most advanced theories, the sources of new knowledge, the broad generalizations which apply to the field as a whole rather than the advanced, highly specialized factual data needed by the teacher of very advanced undergraduate or graduate students.[13]

Surely intelligence and character are important factors in college teaching,[14] though Robert Knapp felt that ". . . the qualities esteemed in the college professor are only secondarily related to his intellectual distinction and primarily to his human and social qualities of personality.[15] It is these human and social qualities that make for rapport, a good environment for learning, and effective communication with students.

[12] American Association of Colleges for Teacher Education, *College Teachers Look at College Teaching*, AACTE Study Series Number 8 (Washington, D.C.: the Association, 1965), p. 87.

[13] Earl J. McGrath, "Superior Teaching in the Colleges of the Sixties," Estrin and Goode, *op. cit.*, p. 553.

[14] Leonard W. Rice, "The Improvement of College Teaching," American Association of Colleges for Teacher Education, *op. cit.*, p. 36.

[15] Knapp, *op. cit.*, p. 304.

Other characteristics that students frequently mention are such things as teaching skill, fairness, sense of humor, and enthusiasm.

Planning is essential for effective college teaching. Every class cannot be "a happening." There are just so many class sessions in a semester, 45 in a three-credit course, for example, and each one should be well planned and purposeful. Some instructors begin a semester without a plan and teach as if there were an unlimited number of classes. Ordway Tead passed on some good advice when he said:

> Let every teacher be sure that every course, and every session of every course, be carefully planned with a beginning, a middle, and an end. And let him engage in self-scrutiny at the end of each day's work to see how class or laboratory performance is really progressing in relation to the plan.[16]

Individual differences are just as important in college teaching as they are in teaching at the lower level. Planning must take individual differences into account. Therefore, varied instruction must be planned to allow for these differences. Assignments must not only be precise and have meaning, but they too must provide for differences in students. We particularly need to help superior students to work at the level of their ability.

We need to plan so that students know where they are going and what is expected of them. They need to see purpose in the work they are doing, and they need the instructor's help in seeing what is important in what they are learning. Unfortunately, some instructors feel that all they need do is offer knowledge; it is up to the student to get this knowledge as best he can. They do not see the student in his own light as a nonspecialist, nor do they distinguish between ". . . the preservation and advancement of knowledge on the one side and education on the other."[17]

A variety of methods should be utilized in the instruction. Too many professors have for too long relied on the lecture method:

[16] Ordway Tead, "Twelve Suggestions for Improving Teaching," Estrin and Goode, *op. cit.*, p. 595.
[17] Joseph Katz, "Personality and Interpersonal Relations in the Classroom," Sanford, *op. cit.*, p. 367.

The role of the teacher has been and will be increasingly altered. The professor whose only skill is to give information will awaken to a realization that there are more effective ways to communicate than by reading a lecture. The teacher of the future will have higher demands placed upon his personality as an inciter, stimulator, motivator, and interpreter. To be able to demonstrate the applicability of information, to solve problems, and to translate facts into significant programs of life and action will be high expectancies of the teacher of the future.[18]

Telling students what they have already read in a textbook is not very effective teaching. It does not place the professor in the role of "inciter, stimulator, motivator, and interpreter." Teaching is surely more than telling.

Discussion can have much value for students. Wilbert McKeachie describes the purposes of this method as:

1. to give students opportunities to formulate principles in their own words and to suggest applications of these principles.
2. to help students become aware of and to define problems based on information derived from readings or lectures.
3. to gain acceptance for information or theories counter to folklore or previous beliefs of students.
4. to get feedback on how well his instructional objectives are being attained.[19]

Among other methods that could be used are laboratory teaching, which has to do with developing skill in observation and ability to apply learning, the project, independent study or the tutorial, and the whole range of automated techniques:

The research to date indicates that television, films, teaching machines, and books can be used to achieve educational objectives. Their usefulness varies depending upon the objectives, the characteristics of the students, and the excellence of their materials. Re-

[18] Samuel D. Marble, "College Teaching Today and Tomorrow: What is Involved?" *Current Issues, 1964,* p. 111.
[19] Wilbert J. McKeachie, "The Discussion Group," *The Delta Pi Epsilon Journal,* 9:1, November, 1966.

search at present reveals no danger that these devices will eliminate the need for face-to-face contacts between professors and students.[20]

Whatever method is used, and there is no evidence that students learn best by any one method, it should provide teaching that is challenging to students, teaching that makes students think, teaching that is interesting for students.

Graduate teaching. In graduate teaching one may be instructing large classes by lecture, directing seminars, or supervising the research of advanced students. Andrew Hacker, in discussing the desire of many professors to teach graduate students, said:

> What is surprising . . . is how many professors are looking forward to when they, too, will be able to restrict their teaching to graduate students. Some have already arrived at this exalted status and more are graduating to it every year.[21]

It is not simply the status of graduate teaching that attracts so many professors, it is also the undesirability of undergraduate teaching:

> Probably the first complaint is the sheer drudgery attending undergraduate classwork. If Original Sin afflicts the teaching profession, its most pronounced manifestation is grading, and—most tiresome of all—penning comments on students' written work. The number of hours consumed in doing even minimal justice to undergraduate examinations and essays may soon get out of hand.[22]

With the expansion of graduate teaching in recent years has come a growing concern for the quality of undergraduate teaching. Many of the best professors have been removed from the undergraduate who is left with lesser professors, outside lecturers, and teaching assistants. Some colleges and universities, though, do make a conscious effort to have the more distinguished professors lecture in basic courses. Hopefully this will become more widespread.

[20] W. J. McKeachie, "Procedures and Techniques of Teaching," Nevitt Sanford, *op. cit.*, p. 351.

[21] Andrew Hacker, "Who Wants to Teach Undergraduates?" *Saturday Review*, December 17, 1966, p. 80.

[22] Hacker, *loc. cit.*

Research and Writing

What is perhaps the best statement that has been made about the whole question of research and other scholarly production by faculty members can be attributed to Logan Wilson:

> Research should have the next priority [after teaching] in many, but by no means all, institutions. In the forseeable future I doubt that our nation needs or can fully support more than 40 or 50 really distinguished, research-oriented universities. Such centers should be more numerous and more widely dispersed than at present, but it is not only wasteful but also futile to think that every locality should aspire to having one or more. Although research of the kind that contributes to the advancement of knowledge should be a major emphasis in perhaps 200 of our institutions, I believe that on most campuses it is sufficient to expect the average faculty member to keep abreast of his field.
>
> Since real creativity in research is a very scarce talent anyhow, I think that most faculty persons would benefit themselves and their institutions more by devoting greater effort to the improvement of teaching. Contrary to the "publish or perish" myth that is much talked about of late, in all except a few leading institutions less than 10 percent of the faculty accounts for 90 percent or more of all published research. My recommendation would be that we reduce the strain on the majority, trim the output of needless publication, and upgrade the quality of instruction by a more realistic adjustment of talents available.[23]

Many faculty members can have satisfying careers without publishing. This is not to imply that they are not scholarly. It may mean that they prefer to devote themselves to teaching and private scholarship. One cannot be a truly effective college teacher without scholarship, but this scholarship need not be the kind that results in publication. Still, it must be granted that some institutions weigh heavily the scholarly production of a professor

[23] Logan Wilson, "Setting Institutional Priorities," *Current Issues, 1965*, p. 38.

for an original appointment or for promotion. Perhaps this is partially due to the fact that articles and books can be read and evaluated, whereas it is difficult to evaluate teaching. One wonders, though, if the evaluation of printed material cannot be just as subjective as the evaluation of teaching.

Working with Students

The college faculty member works with students in and out of class. Students are the college in a very real sense, for "if students come to the university to learn, and if the institutions of higher learning are supported so that students will learn, then students are the most important ingredient in the university. . . ."[24] Time spent working with students is not "wasted time," as some faculty seem to feel; it is part of their job.

The professor should be an effective counselor of students, for they will bring a great range of problems to discuss. He will have to learn to listen well to students, and not just with his ears. More importantly, he will have to learn when he is beyond his depth—when he should refer the student to one more qualified to help. The average professor is not a therapist and should not attempt to give therapy. The emotional life of the student is too valuable and vulnerable to be tampered with.

Students need very much to be helped to be more self-directing. If all decisions are made for them, if no option is left open, there is little room for growth. On the other hand, if they receive no help, no guidance, they can at best flounder; at worst they can make some costly errors. It is difficult to steer a path between providing too much help and not providing enough. This, however, is effective counseling.

It is most important to get to know students, but it is not always easy to do so. If an instructor has a student load of 150 and wishes to have a ten-minute conference with each student, it will require over 21 hours to complete just this one round of conferences! The instructor may decide to get to know students simply

---

[24] American Association of Colleges for Teacher Education, *op. cit.*, p. 93.

through classwork. This is difficult, particularly if his major teaching method is lecture.

Some instructors just do not know their students. Yet, there is nothing more disconcerting than to look at a name in a grade book at the end of a semester and not know who it is. Is it the student with black hair who sat in the back of the room, or is it the tall boy who sat in front? Just how grades are assigned in these circumstances is a bit of a mystery.

It should be unnecessary to say that students should be treated with respect, but unfortunately they are not always so treated. Ridicule and sarcasm have no place in the faculty member's relationship with students in or out of the classroom.

Students want to be treated as persons, as individuals. Despite the fact that they try to keep their "cool" outwardly, students do care; they want personal contacts with faculty. They do not want to be viewed simply as names in a grade book or numbers on an IBM card.

Academic Service

The professor spends much time in the area of academic service. There are faculty, divisional, and departmental meetings to attend; there are student activities and organizations to be sponsored; and then there are the committees. Beyond this, there may be other activities directly or indirectly connected with the college in which faculty members are active.

Professors, as any student knows, like to talk. This propensity for verbalization can make not only for meetings that are long, but it can also make for many meetings. Nowhere is this more apparent than at committee meetings where a great deal of time can be consumed discussing one minor point. At the next meeting of the committee, the very same point may be raised for continued discussion.

The role of the faculty in the governance of institutions of higher education varies greatly. In one institution there may be a representative faculty group impowered to make decisions; in another, the faculty is not involved in decision-making at all; in still another, the faculty is given the impression of being involved through much committee work when, in fact, they have little to say. Of the three varieties mentioned, the last is probably the most frustrating because of so much wasted motion, lost time, and sham. Whatever the form of governance, faculty time is involved.

Professional Activities

Part of keeping professionally alive and keeping up with one's field involves attending professional meetings and conferences, workshops or seminars, leaves for teaching at other institutions, for research, for travel, or perhaps for further study.

Some faculty members, who become active participants in meetings of their discipline group or national groups concerned with higher education, prepare papers to be read or participate in panel discussions. Again, these are time-consuming activities but a part of the professor's work.

Other Activities

There are things that faculty members do beyond what has been described above. Some professors serve as consultants to business or government, for example. Some are concerned with editing or reviewing new written material. Many are involved in community service, which may mean speaking to the PTA or League of Women Voters, or serving in some advisory capacity to a civic group. There are, then, activities beyond the regular "job" that call for the professor's time.

TEACHING IN THE COMMUNITY COLLEGE

Nature of the Community College

The junior or community college is normally a two-year institution designed to meet local needs, and it usually features low tuition. It offers programs in general and terminal education as well as providing educational programs for adults. Students who pursue the two-year general education course, comparable to the first two years of college, earn the Associate in Arts degree. Many of these youngsters then transfer to a four-year institution to complete the bachelor's degree. The community college thus provides the opportunity for many to complete four years of college who otherwise would not be able to do so. Remaining at home and paying low tuition for the first two years, the student frequently can afford the cost of the last two years of college.

In the terminal programs, technical and semi-professional education is provided. For example, there may be programs in mechanical, electrical, and medical technology; there may be secretarial or accounting programs; or there may be programs in advertising, hotel technology, or retail distribution. These programs prepare students at the level of technician, for example, not at the level of engineer. And they may be two years, one year, or shorter in length. The important point is that they provide programs beyond high school to meet community needs.

There is some difference of opinion as to whether the community or junior college is part of higher education or an extension of the secondary school. Both points of view have their advocates. The author tends to see the institution as a part of higher education, though many community colleges are linked with local school boards and high school administration. Perhaps more time will have to pass, though, before a firm decision can be made. The community college is still growing so rapidly (some 40 states are now preparing plans for public junior colleges) that the picture is not completely clear. If the institution does not develop along collegiate lines, the opportunity for general education students to transfer to four-year colleges may be impeded.

The Work of the Community College Teacher

The principal work of the community college teacher is *teaching*. And this is properly so.

> The first specific goal of the junior college is quality teaching. While the college exists to serve students and couldn't exist without them, its heart is the faculty. Students are transitory, the faculty is permanent. . . . The difference between a good and a poor junior

college is the quality of teaching that is done. Effective teaching is and must remain the paramount goal of junior colleges.[25]

These, then, are teaching institutions and the priority assigned to teaching is apparent.

The faculty member's teaching load would tend to be higher in the community college than in the four-year college, though his salary, over a period of years, would probably not be.[26] There would be little or no demand for research and/or scholarly production. Thus, the community college teacher has more time to put into his teaching.

The normal work would be at least 15 teaching hours. Several teaching preparations could be expected. And ample time would have to be set aside for counseling students. The community college is one place where the student should be able to find superior counseling. For it is here that he may make some important decision: Has he selected the proper curriculum? Is he really suited for the field of his choice? Should he go on to the four-year college or university? With all of these decisions the student needs help. Such decisions may well affect the rest of his life.

The community colleges are not without their problems. Perhaps the most pressing problem is quality teaching:

> I see no greater single problem facing junior college teachers than the upgrading of the people who are already on our faculties; and the attracting to our kinds of colleges the best young teachers available.[27]

Perhaps new programs are needed to prepare and upgrade community college teachers. The program instituted by Yale University leading to a new degree, Master of Philosophy, is illustra-

[25] Charles E. Chapman, "Aligning Priorities in Junior and Community Colleges," *Current Issues, 1965*, p. 167.

[26] See, for example, Peggy Heim and William Baumol, "Salary Structures in Public Junior Colleges Which Do Not Have the Usual Academic Ranks, 1965–66," *AAUP Bulletin*, 52:401–407, December, 1966.

[27] Roger H. Garrison, "Professional Teacher or Dedicated Amateur?" *School and Society*, 93:392, October 30, 1965.

tive. To earn the degree, a student completes all the requirements for the Ph. D. with the exception of the dissertation. The purpose is to prepare more college teachers who are liberally educated at the graduate level but not necessarily research oriented. It would also help to salvage a number of candidates for the Ph.D. who never do complete the dissertation.

We have tried to present a picture of what it is like to teach at the college level. To be a professor, one should have decidedly above-average talents and be attracted to and interested in the academic life. Furthermore, one must be willing to make quite a commitment:

> It is a remarkable thing to which we commit ourselves when we become college teachers—the commitment to remain intellectually alive at least until we reach retirement. It is like committing to love through sickness and health, poverty and prosperity. To stay intellectually alive is an exhausting task.[28]

Though the work of the college teacher is difficult and taxing, it does provide challenge and satisfaction.

SUGGESTED ACTIVITIES

1. Interview several of your college-going friends in order to determine why they have come to college and what they think of their experience so far. Bring your findings to class for discussion.
2. Visit the campus of another college. Talk to students and faculty and observe some classes if possible. In what ways is this college different from your own?
3. What are the characteristics of the effective college teachers you have noticed so far? The ineffective?
4. Form a committee to plan and present a panel discussion on today's college student.
5. Arrange a debate on who should attend college.
6. Investigate what has been done in your state to meet the growing need for higher education.

[28] Leonard W. Rice, "The Improvement of College Teaching," American Association of Colleges for Teacher Education," op. cit., pp. 37–38.

7. Consult several junior or community college catalogues to determine the variety of programs offered by this type of institution.
8. Find out the requirements of several graduate schools in the area of
your interest.
9. Interview several faculty members on the advantages and disadvantages of college teaching as a career.

SELECTED REFERENCES

American Association of Colleges for Teacher Education. *College
Teachers Look at College Teaching*. AACTE Study Series, Number
8. Washington, D.C.: the Association, 1965. A report by the Subcommittee on the Improvement of Instruction of the Committee on
Studies. The report contains the results of two seminars of outstanding faculty members conducted by the Subcommittee and suggestions for the improvement of college teaching.

Association for Higher Education. *Current Issues in Higher Education,
1964. Undergraduate Education*. Washington, D.C.: Association for
Higher Education, National Education Association, 1964. The proceedings of the nineteenth annual national conference on higher education, April 19–20, 1964, dealing with some of the issues and
trends in undergraduate education.

Association for Higher Education. *Current Issues in Higher Education,
1965. Pressures and Priorities in Higher Education*. Washington,
D.C.: Association for Higher Education, National Education Association, 1965. The proceedings of the twentieth annual national conference on higher education, March 7–10, 1965, dealing with issues
and trends related to the theme of the conference.

Baskin, Samuel, ed. *Higher Education: Some New Developments*.
New York: McGraw-Hill Book Company, 1965. Informative papers
on recent changes in college and university instruction and administration.

Brickman, William B., and Lehrer, Stanley, eds. *A Century of Higher
Education*. New York: Society for the Advancement of Education,
1962. Writings concerning a history of higher education in which all
types of colleges and universities are included.

Carmichael, Oliver C. *Graduate Education: A Critique and a Program*.
New York: Harper & Row, Publishers, 1961. The weaknesses of

graduate education and ways and means of their correction are discussed.

Estrin, Herman A., and Goode, Delmer M., eds. *College and University Teaching*. Dubuque, Iowa: Wm. C. Brown Company Publishers, 1964. A compilation of 122 articles dealing with various phases of college teaching selected from the journal *Improving College and University Teaching*.

Fields, Ralph R. *The Community College Movement*. New York: McGraw-Hill Book Company, 1962. Four case descriptions of community colleges are given as well as the historical picture of the movement.

Lloyd-Jones, Ester, and Estrin, Herman A. *The American Student and His College*. Boston: Houghton Mifflin, 1967. A number of selections dealing with college life. Current concerns such as students' rights and responsibilities are probed.

Rosencrance, Francis C. *The American College and its Teachers*. New York: The Macmillan Company, 1962. Considers the opportunities, functions, and responsibilities of the college teacher.

Sanford, Nevitt, ed. *The American College*. New York: John Wiley & Sons, 1963. A lengthy and scholarly "psychological and social interpretation of the higher learning." Part III, "Academic Procedures," has much information of value concerning college teaching.

Thornton, James W. *The Community Junior College*. Second edition. New York: John Wiley & Sons, 1966. Considers the backgrounds, organization, and operation of the community junior college as well as issues and opportunities.

6 The American Public School System

While the focus in this volume is on teaching, an introduction to education would be incomplete without an examination of the American public school system. It is within this system that you as a public school teacher will work. You should know something of how this system developed, how it is organized, and how it is financed. An attempt to provide you with this knowledge will be made in this chapter, though in an introductory book it is not possible to go deeply into these topics. Here, an overview will be presented with the hope that you will pursue further knowledge in subsequent study.[1]

HISTORICAL DEVELOPMENT

As one views the American public school system today and sees the vastness of this enterprise, it may seem difficult to believe that its development was not really well planned. It perhaps is not even accurate to speak of the American public school system, for in reality there are a number of "systems" within the system; it is probably more accurate to speak of the American educational system. How did this system develop?

---

[1] At the end of this chapter, a number of sources are listed for further reading.

Colonial Period (1620–1775)

The New England colonies. The views of the Puritans who settled in New England markedly affected the development of education in these colonies. Since religion was the center of Puritan
life, it was also the center of their educational concerns. So, too, it
was difficult to distinguish between Church and State.

In 1642, the Commonwealth of Massachusetts enacted a law
that made parents responsible for the education of their children.
The law established no schools, but simply empowered the
officials of each town to ascertain whether parents were fulfilling
their duties. However, in 1647 the famous "Old Deluder Satan
Act" was passed. This law required that towns having fifty householders establish reading and writing schools; towns having one
hundred or more householders had to establish Latin grammar
schools. Thus, important principles were set forth:

> . . . the state could require children to be educated; the state could
> require towns to establish schools; the civil government could super-
> vise and control schools by direct management in the hands of
> public officials; and public funds could be used for the support of
> public schools.[2]

The reading and writing schools were taught by a traveling
schoolmaster and were for young children. The youngsters were
taught to read so that they could read the Bible and the Cate-
chism. The principles of the Christian religion were taught by the
schoolmaster. Latin grammar schools, the first secondary schools,
prepared for college. Instruction in the colonial colleges such as
Harvard was in Latin and Greek, for these colleges were dedicated to preparing ministers. In addition to the reading and writing schools, there were the "dame schools." In these schools a
woman taught her own children and others in the neighborhood
some reading, perhaps some writing, and some household skills.

[2] R. Freeman Butts and Lawrence A. Cremin, *A History of Education in American Culture* (New York: Holt, Rinehart and Winston, copyright 1953), p. 103.

By teaching these primary children in her home, she could earn a small amount of money per week.

The middle colonies. The middle colonies were settled by a diversity of religious groups. Each of these groups wanted to provide education in its own religious schools. So, in the middle colonies too there were parochial schools, though they were not aligned with the State as in New England.

A distinct contribution of the middle colonies was the academy, the first of which was founded by Benjamin Franklin in Philadelphia in 1751. The academies were important because they attempted to provide a more practical kind of education than did the Latin grammar school. Such subjects as surveying, bookkeeping, stenography, and navigation were taught. They attempted to prepare for life as well as the ministry; they enrolled students not going to college as well as the college bound. Later on, they permitted young women to enter.

The southern colonies. Anglicans settled in the southern colonies and brought with them the English aristocratic concept of education—education was largely a private matter or a matter to be taken care of by the Church, though Church and State were not joined as they were in New England.

The apprenticeship system, through which a boy learned a trade taught by a master, was used. There was also the "charity school" conducted by the Church for pauper children. However, many children of the well-to-do planters were tutored and sent to private schools or back to England for further education. The College of William and Mary, established at Williamsburg, Virginia in 1693, provided higher education in the southern colonies.

The Early National Period (1776–1825)

The Northwest Ordinance, first enacted by Congress in 1785 and reaffirmed in 1787, set forth the regulations for settling the vast western territories, and it provided that "there shall be reserved the lot number sixteen of every township for the maintenance of public schools within the township." This grant of federal lands for school use represents the first enactment of federal aid for education.

Thomas Jefferson's concept of education was a radical one for that time. He proposed that all receive a basic elementary education and that the brighter children be given a chance to go on to secondary and higher education. His ideas, however, were not adopted by the Virginia legislature. He also labored long and hard for the establishment of the University of Virginia, which was founded in 1819.

The Dartmouth College Decision of 1819 was an important one. New Hampshire had attempted to take over Dartmouth College, a private institution. The United States Supreme Court ruled that Dartmouth had a right to exist under its charter. Not only was this case significant for private education, but it was also significant for public education. If states wanted institutions that they could control and administer, they would have to establish them.

It was during this period and for the next quarter century that the academies were most popular. The first public high schools, however, were founded at this time. In 1821, the first public high school was founded in Boston. This school was for boys, but a school for girls was founded in the same city in 1826. Another fifty years were to pass, though, before the public high school would come into its own.

Formative Period, Common School Revival (1826–1860)

Horace Mann did monumental work to bring about the ideal of the common school,[3] a public school for all children. He and such men as Henry Barnard and Caleb Mills led the battle for the free elementary school open to all. It may seem strange today to say that people of this period were opposed to the free public school, but many were. There were enough people who believed that the only proper education was a religious education; there were those who believed that their taxes should not be used to educate the

[3] Among other things Horace Mann did was to establish the first state normal school in Massachusetts in 1839.

children of others; and there were those who believed that well-to-do children should not attend the same school as as the children of ordinary citizens. Other groups had other reasons for their opposition, all of which made for quite a battle. The battle ultimately was won for the free elementary school—Pennsylvania, in 1834, became the first state to adopt a program of free schools.

The monitorial school, developed by the Englishman Joseph Lancaster, was in vogue for part of this period. It was a system whereby up to a thousand students could be taught at one time through the use of monitors. The master teacher would teach the monitors the lesson. They, in turn, would teach the lesson and administer the punishments to their groups of ten students or so. The method was popular for a while because it seemed to be an inexpensive way of educating large numbers of students. However, there were too many built-in problems, such as rigidity and too much mechanization, for the method to be successful.

A number of state universities were established in this era, and the turn away from religion and the classics toward science and the professions began.

American Education Comes of Age (1865–1957)

The First Morrill Act of 1862 was a great boon to higher education. It provided the states with federal land to be sold to raise funds for the establishment of colleges of agricultural and mechanical arts. All of the land-grant colleges stem from this and subsequent Morrill Acts.

As the battle for the free public elementary school had been fought some fifty years before, now the battle for the public high school was raging. It was finally settled by the Kalamazoo Decision in 1874. The Supreme Court of Michigan ruled that communities could tax themselves for the support of public high schools. It paved the way for the tremendous growth in high school enrollments (from 132,000 in 1880 to over 16,000,000 by 1967).

In this period the elementary schools, which were also expanding greatly in enrollment, became graded schools. Not all elementary schools were eight-year schools; some were seven- and some nine-year. There was originally no set plan to have eight years of elementary school and four years of high school.

At this time, too, the first public kindergarten was founded in St. Louis in 1873, under Superintendent William T. Harris. It stemmed from the work first done by Friedrich Froebel in Germany.

There was further development and expansion of the normal schools—two-year institutions for preparing teachers—and Teachers College of Columbia University was established in 1888. In the 1920's and 30's most normal schools became three- and four-year collegiate institutions.

A period of studying education by national committees began in these years. For example, the Committee of Ten, appointed in 1892, recommended that elementary education be confined to six years and that seventh and eighth grades be concerned with secondary education. The junior high school and the junior college were originated in recommendations of the Committee on the Economy of Time in Education in 1911.

Progressive education began to emerge in this country with the work of John Dewey and Colonel Francis Parker, principal of the Cook County Normal School in Chicago. From its beginning and even throughout the height of its popularity, progressive education was much misunderstood. It never meant, for example, that children should be able to do just what they wanted to do—probably many of them would have wanted to go home; it never meant that there should be no discipline. Just what did progressive education mean? One of the best definitions was given by Lawrence A. Cremin:

> First, it meant broadening the program and function of the school to include direct concern for health, vocation, and the quality of family and community life.
>
> Second, it meant applying in the classroom the pedagogical principles derived from new scientific research in psychology and the social sciences.
>
> Third, it meant tailoring instruction more and more to the different kinds and classes of children who were being brought within the

purview of the school. . . . For if everyone was to attend school, the Progressives contended, not only the methods but the very meaning of education would have to change. . . .

Finally, Progressivism implied the radical faith that culture could be democratized without being vulgarized, the faith that everyone could share not only in the benefits of the new sciences but in the pursuit of the arts as well.[4]

Through compulsory education laws, the schools now had practically "all of the children of all of the people" attending. Questions of grouping and promotion were raised: Should youngsters be grouped homogeneously? Would homogeneous grouping produce better educational results than heterogeneous grouping? Should children be promoted so as to keep them with their agemates or because they attain certain educational standards? Does a student really get that much out of repeating a grade or subject? There are still no definitive answers to all of these questions.

The schools in this period embarked upon a testing program and the scientific study of education growing out of the work of men like Thorndike, Binet, and Judd. Intelligence tests began to be used in the schools after their first large-scale use in World War I. The IQ, intelligence quotient, came into use. It represented the relationship of a child's chronological age and mental age on a base of 100. For example, if a ten-year-old child performs as well as a twelve-year-old child on a given test, his IQ would be 120—twelve tenths of 100.

The junior high school went through a period of great growth, and the elementary school became more child-centered: an attempt was made to fit the school to the child rather than the child to the school. Schools became more concerned with real-life problems and attempted to implement this concern through revitalized curricula. There was interest in life-adjustment education.

The historic decision of the United States Supreme Court in 1954 that "separate facilities were inherently unequal" had great

[4] Lawrence A. Cremin, *The Transformation of the School* (New York: Alfred A. Knopf, 1961), pp. vii–ix.

implications for education. The long struggle began to bring about integrated schooling for Negro children.

Period of Re-evaluation and Analysis (1957–   )

Demarking recent history is arbitrary, but it does seem as if a radical change began to take place in the schools after the launching of the first Sputnik. The schools were subjected to severe criticism, particularly in the area of curriculum. This caused a greater emphasis to be placed on science and mathematics; less attention was given to the humanities. The emphasis was placed more heavily on academic achievement as more and more youngsters went on to college.

Attention was focused on *de facto* segregation, not merely on *de jure* segregation. Various plans were instituted to bring about integration: pairing schools, permissive bussing, and open enrollment, for example. The schools still struggle with the problem.

The question of religion and the public schools became even more controversial as the result of several Supreme Court decisions, particularly the decision that Bible reading and reciting the Lord's Prayer could no longer take place in the public school. The Court said that the schools could "teach about religion," but many people felt that God had been taken out of the school. Though the law has been more clearly delineated, the controversy continues.

Enrollments continued to increase, and the whole range of automated techniques for teaching received even more attention. Language laboratories, teaching by television, and programed learning were experimented with. Federal aid to education was much increased through the Elementary and Secondary Education Act of 1965, which authorized $1.3 billion in benefits to elementary and secondary schools.

ORGANIZATION AND FINANCE OF PUBLIC EDUCATION

At the National Level

There is no mention of education in the Constitution, but justification for concern and support by the federal government is found in the "general welfare" clause of the Constitution. There was to be no centralized system, so education was left in the hands of the states by the Tenth Amendment, which said that: "The powers not delegated to the United States by the Constitution, nor prohibited by it to the states, are reserved to the states respectively, or to the people."

From its beginnings the federal government has supported education through various grants and funds. The *Northwest Ordinance* and the first *Morrill Act,* discussed earlier in the chapter, are examples of such aid. Other important instances of federal involvement in education are:

Smith-Hughes Act of 1917—This act provided funds for vocational education in the secondary school. The appropriations were for teachers and supervisors of agriculture, home economics, trade and industrial subjects; for teacher training in these subjects; and for studies in vocational education. States had to match federal funds, a principle established in the Smith-Lever Act of 1914.

The GI Bill of Rights—Appropriations permitted the veterans of World War II and subsequent veterans to further their education. Many veterans were able to secure college educations as a result of the Bill.

U.S. Supreme Court Decision on Desegregation in 1954—The Court held that racial segregation in the public schools violated the U.S. Constitution.

The National Defense Education Act of 1958—Under this act, and its subsequent renewals, funds were provided for loans and fellowships for college students; for equipment for and teaching of science, math, and foreign languages; for guidance, counseling, and testing in elementary and secondary schools; for various research projects; and for improving state education agencies.

U.S. Supreme Court Decision on Bible Reading and the Lord's Prayer in 1963—The Court declared that Bible reading and the recitation of the Lord's Prayer in public schools were unconstitutional on the grounds that these were religious exercises and, thus, violated the "establishment of religion" clause of the First Amendment to the Constitution.

Economic Opportunity Act of 1964—This part of the "War Against Poverty" provided part-time employment for needy college students and literacy programs for adults to help them gain employment. Other important educational aspects of this act were the Head Start Program and the Job Corps. The purpose of the well-known Head Start Program is to provide socially and culturally deprived children with a "head start" through enriched preschool programs. The Job Corps furnishes basic education and vocational training for dropouts and potential dropouts.

The Elementary and Secondary Education Act of 1965—Under the several titles of this act, financial assistance is given to local education agencies for the education of children of low-income families; for school library resources and instructional materials (these materials may be loaned to non-public schools); for supplementary educational centers and services such as educational television, remedial instruction, and guidance and counseling; for educational research and training; and for strengthening state departments of education.

The U.S. Office of Education, under the Department of Health, Education, and Welfare, is the agency responsible for most, though not all, of the federal government's concerns and activities in education. The Office, directed by a Commissioner, conducts research, administers grants, and provides services to other agencies at the local, state, national, and international levels. In recent years the Commissioner has also had the responsibility of ascertaining that school districts complied with the guidelines established for desegregation before these districts received federal funds. This responsibility, however, was shifted to the Office of Civil Rights in the Department of Health, Education, and Welfare in 1967.

A reorganization of the Department of Health, Education, and Welfare is being considered by its Secretary. The Department may be divided into three subordinate departments under secretaries who would report directly to the Health, Education, and

Welfare secretary. Currently, there is an Assistant Secretary for Education.

In addition to operating the military academies such as the U.S. Military Academy (West Point) and the Naval Academy, the federal government also operates schools for the children of servicemen throughout the world. These activities, along with those listed above and others too numerous to detail here,[5] illustrate the extent to which the federal government is involved in education.

There are those who believe that the federal government has not gone far enough in its support of education. They believe that there should be more general aid to help equalize educational opportunity among the states. Furthermore, the federal government is in a better position than the states to secure funds through taxation:

> The concerted national effort to provide public schools that will serve more students more effectively has been frustrated by the inherent inadequacies of state and local tax systems. Although thousands of local tax elections have authorized increased school property tax rates in recent years and state legislatures have increased state tax rates, the process has failed to produce revenues needed to accommodate the rising enrollments and *at the same time* provide more and better educational services.[6]

At the State Level

As noted earlier, education is a function of state government because of the Tenth Amendment to the U.S. Constitution. A typical organization for education at the state level will be reviewed here, though there are variations.

The state legislature enacts broad educational policy; that is, it establishes the laws providing for and governing education. Thus, it is the ultimate source of authority over education in the state.

[5] There were, for example, seventeen different education programs established in the first thirty-one months of the Johnson administration.

[6] American Association of School Administrators, *The Federal Government and Public Schools* (Washington, D.C.: the Association, 1965), p. 53.

The state board of education, as it is called in some states, for-
mulates educational policy within the framework established by
the legislature. The board is usually appointed by the governor,
though board members are elected in some states.

The state board, in turn, may appoint the chief state school officer, though he is still elected by popular vote in most states. His
title varies (it may be Commissioner of Education or Superintendent of Public Instruction, for example), but his function is the
same—chief executive officer of the state board of education.

The state department of education, under the direction of the
commissioner of education, carries out the policy established by
the state board of education. The staff of the department, which
may be sizable, assists the commissioner in fulfilling the department's leadership, regulatory, and operational functions.

In any discussion of the state organization of education, the
courts must be included. Though the courts are not part of the
educational system, they are most important in the scheme of
things. In our country, the law is what the courts say it is. The
validity of a law is not known until it is tested. Thus, many educational controversies have been settled in the courts.

Through the mechanism outlined above, the state performs its
educational functions. Among these functions are coordination of
all education within the state, establishment of minimum standards, preparation of a plan of financial support, and provision of
consultative services.

State financing of education. On the average, state governments provide 40 percent of the revenue for public elementary
and secondary schools.[7] The range is from a high of 77.7 percent
for Delaware to a low of 4.7 percent for Nebraska.[8] Therefore,
while every state supports education, there is great variation in
the amount of that support.

What should be the objectives of a good program of state sup-

[7] National Education Association, Research Division, *Estimates of School
Statistics, 1964–65,* Research Report 1964-R17 (Washington, D.C.: the
Association, 1964), p. 29.

[8] National Education Association, *loc. cit.*

port of education? The National Education Association suggests the following:

1. Educational opportunity should be provided for all children and youth by establishing an adequate minimum or foundation of financial support per pupil in all school districts.
2. Local interest and initiative in education should be preserved by requiring all local districts to make an equitable contribution toward the financing of schools in terms of local financial ability.
3. The required local contribution should be such as to leave tax leeway in the community available for local innovation and experimentation in the schools.
4. The cost of the schools should be equitably distributed over all forms of taxable capacity.
5. The total amount available for the schools should be sufficient to permit the financing of a quality program of education.[9]

Through the basic program advocated above, every boy and girl in the state should be given the opportunity to receive an education that does not fall below the minimum established by the program. Because a youngster is born in a financially less favored section of the state, he should not be deprived of at least that minimum education.

The state is in a position to collect the taxes where they are available and spend the funds where the pupils are located through the use of the equalization principle. In any state, there are bound to be areas that are not as capable of supporting education as are other areas. The equalization principle takes into account the ability of the local community to support education in determining the distribution of state aid. Suppose that the state minimum program is set at $450 per pupil per year. Community A with $3,000 of property valuation per pupil assesses at 20 percent of the real value of the property. The $3,000 is multiplied by 5 to get the true value of $15,000 per pupil. Community B with $25,000 of property valuation per pupil assesses at 50 percent of

[9] National Education Association, Research Division, *What Everyone Should Know About Financing Our Schools* (Washington, D.C.: the Association, 1966), p. 47. Original in italics.

full value (not all communities in the state assess property at the same percent of true or full value). The $25,000 is multiplied by 2 to get the true value of $50,000 per pupil. Next, a uniform and reasonable tax rate is set by the state, based upon full valuation. Suppose it is $7 per thousand of full property value. This rate will raise $105 per pupil in community A ($7 per thousand times $15,000) and $350 per pupil in community B ($7 per thousand times $50,000). The state then furnishes Community A with $345 per pupil, the difference between the foundation program of $450 per pupil and the $105 per pupil the community can reasonably raise. By the same procedure, Community B would receive $100 per pupil. This computation is made for each community, thus assuring a more equal distribution of the cost of education in the state.

At the Local Level

Though education is a function of the state, operational responsibility for the schools is placed at the local level. Throughout our history, we have had a tradition of strong local control of schools.

The local board of education is the policy-making body for the school district. Not only is it a local authority, but it is also an arm of the state. These boards, which are usually elected, vary in size, though they tend to be no larger than nine members. They should, however, have enough members to represent the various points of view in the community. Usually the legal qualifications for membership are at a bare minimum—a certain residency requirement and twenty-one years of age, for example. The kinds of qualities one would desire in a school board member, nevertheless, could entail quite a long list. Among these qualities would be such things as integrity, dedication, sound judgment, and courage.

The powers and functions of boards of education are many. They make policies to develop and improve the educational program; they provide funds and facilities; they select the superintendent; they employ the staff on the recommendation of the superintendent; they approve the daily schedule; and they select school sites, usually with state approval. These are only some of their powers and functions.

The superintendent of schools, appointed by the board of education, is the chief administrative officer for the school district. His responsibilities are many and demanding.[10] He must administer the educational program, finance and facilities, and personnel, and he must promote good school–community relations. Not only must he be an outstanding educator and administrator to be really successful, but he must also be skilled in human relations. Much of the time he deals with people, and the outcome of these relations will influence how effectively and efficiently the school system operates.

The principal is the educational leader of his school. He is the link between the superintendent and the teachers. While he has many duties, his work with the staff and the program is most important. He should be on hand to assist and encourage teachers. Unfortunately, some principals just don't get out of their offices enough. One youngster thought the principal was the man who called fire drills because this was the only time the child ever saw him!

In large school systems, there are many administrative and supervisory positions as well as specialists in various fields like speech therapy, reading, art, and music. Many of the specialists perform *staff* functions rather than *line* functions as do administrators. *Line* refers to a direct line of authority as exists between the principal and his teachers; *staff* refers to a cooperative relationship as would exist between the classroom teacher and the art specialist.

Local financing of education. The community, through its board of education, determines the kind of educational program it wishes to have. The board must then prepare a budget that will support such a program. The budget, in most cases, is submitted

---

[10] For a more detailed discussion of the functions of both the superintendent and the principal, see Chapter 8, "Careers in Education."

to the people for approval. If the public approves the budget, the board then may go ahead and spend the funds for the kind of program the community has supported.

Where does the money come from? Some small proportion of the money comes from the federal government; about 40 percent comes from state aid, as noted earlier; and the bulk of the money comes from local property taxes. In recent years, however, local property taxes in some areas have risen almost to the point where they can be no higher. Additional aid from state and federal governments is needed to relieve the burden on the local taxpayer.

The local school taxes on real property are determined in the following way. After the board of education has decided upon the amount of its budget to be raised through local taxation, that amount is divided by the amount of the total assessed value of real property in the community. The result is the tax rate, $8 per $1,000 of assessed value, for example. This rate is applied to all taxable real property. Thus, the tax share of a homeowner whose house was valued at $12,000 would be $96.

Teachers should be involved in the preparation of the suggested budget presented by the superintendent to the board, and more teachers than ever before are involved in budget preparation today. Teachers are not only concerned with salary provisions in the budget, but as taxpayers they are concerned with its general provisions. In many ways, furthermore, it is the teachers who will implement a good part of the budget right in their classrooms.

The question is often asked, "Why does education cost so much?" There are three principal reasons: (1) inflation—every year it costs more to pay for the same quality of education provided last year; (2) increased enrollments—more and more boys and girls need to be educated each year; and (3) increased quality—schools need to provide better programs and services, if progress is to be made, and this costs more. Added to this push for quality must be the cost of attempting to bring teachers' salaries to a point where people of high quality will be attracted to and remain in the teaching profession.

Why is it that many school budgets do not provide for high-quality education?

The typical budget authorizes less than is needed to provide first-rate schooling for all pupils. This is to be expected from procedures usually followed. Estimates are made of minimum financial needs of the schools. These estimates are then cut to take account of estimated revenues, these being limited by ability or assumed willingness to pay, arbitrary tax limits, under-assessment of property, inequitable sharing in school costs by state and federal governments, and other obstacles to adequate support. Even this minimum budget may be further cut in communities where review by some other agencies determines the final amount. This procedure year after year is at the root of inadequate school support in many communities.[11]

How can one determine whether a school budget is sufficient to finance quality education? The National Education Association offers the following list of points to consider in seeking an answer to such a question:

1. What class size will the budget finance? Does it contemplate individual or mass instruction?
2. Will the budget provide modern instructional materials?
3. Does it provide for specialists to aid teachers in improving instruction?
4. Is there provision for developing instructional programs to meet the needs of certain special groups, such as the culturally deprived, the physically handicapped, the slow learners, and the academically talented?
5. Is there provision for counseling and guidance programs to aid pupils and parents in planning educational and vocational careers?
6. Is the salary schedule one which will attract and hold quality teachers—one which pays beginning and average salaries comparable to those paid other professionals in the region?
7. Is a summer school provided to meet the special needs of those

[11] National Education Association, Research Division, *What Everyone Should Know About Financing Our Schools* (Washington, D.C.: the Association, 1966), pp. 32–33.

who would otherwise be required to repeat a grade at a full year's cost, of pupils qualified to make an extra grade, and of highly gifted pupils?

8. Is there provision for a program using school buildings as community centers, and for the recreation activities using school playgrounds after school and during the summer vacation?

9. Is there a sufficient number of fully qualified school administrators to provide the school system with dynamic leadership?

10. Is there a program for the orientation of new employees?

11. Is a penny-wise and pound-foolish policy being avoided by making school-plant repairs and improvements as needed to increase the schools' attractiveness, safety, and general educational effectiveness?

12. Is there a long-term plan for meeting future school-plant needs, including the purchase of desirable sites readily available now but likely to be available only at prohibitive costs if purchases are too long deferred?[12]

If such questions as those above can be answered in the affirmative, the budget will go a long way toward financing quality education.

This discussion of the historical development and the organization and finance of the American public school system has been brief. It is only a beginning, an introduction. Subsequent study is necessary in order to provide the kind of knowledge you should have to be part of that system as a professional teacher.

SUGGESTED ACTIVITIES

1. Select a current educational problem and trace its historical development in American education.

2. Investigate some of the highlights of the historical development of education in your state and present your findings to the class.

3. Prepare a report on several Supreme Court cases that have had a marked effect upon education in our country. Be sure to point out ways in which they influenced education.

[12] *Ibid.*, pp. 33–34. Original in italics.

4. Form a committee to present a panel discussion of the pros and cons of further federal financial aid to education.
5. Determine, with regard to the state commissioner or state superintendent of education, the qualifications, term of office, salary, and duties of the position.
6. Visit a local school board meeting.
7. Interview a school board member concerning his responsibilities as a member of the board.
8. Find out how parochial and private schools are financed in your state.

SELECTED REFERENCES

American Association of School Administrators. *The Federal Government and Public Schools.* Washington, D.C.: the Association, 1965. Examines the problems and issues growing out of the changing relationships among various levels of government as they affect public schools.

Brubacher, John S. *A History of the Problems of Education.* Second edition. New York: McGraw-Hill Book Company, 1966. A good reference on issues and problems in education.

Butts, R. Freeman, and Cremin, Lawrence A. *A Hisory of Education in American Culture.* New York: Holt, Rinehart and Winston, 1953. An excellent reference on the past in American education as it relates to present and future problems.

Callahan, Raymond E. *An Introduction to Education in American Society.* Second edition. New York: Alfred A. Knopf, 1964. See Chapter 6, "The History of American Education," and Chapter 17, "History of the Teaching Profession in America."

Cremin, Lawrence A. *Transformation of the School.* New York: Alfred A. Knopf, 1961. A fine and accurate history of the progressive education movement.

Cubberley, Ellwood P. *Public Education in the United States.* Boston: Houghton Mifflin Company, 1934. A lengthy but classic reference on the history of American education.

DeYoung, Chris A., and Wynn, Richard. *American Education.* Fifth edition. New York: McGraw-Hill Book Company, 1964. For a more detailed consideration of the organization and administration of education, see Part II of this volume; for school finance see Chapter 17.

Good, Harry G. *A History of American Education.* Second edition. New York: The Macmillan Co., 1962. A comprehensive treatment of the development of American education.

Meyer, Adolphe E. *An Educational History of the American People.* Second edition. New York: McGraw-Hill Book Company, 1967. A scholarly documentation of American educational history.

National Education Association, Research Division. *What Everyone Should Know About Financing Our Schools.* Washington, D.C.: the Association, 1966. A good primer on school finance.

National Education Association, Special Project on School Finance. *Financing the Public Schools, 1960–1970.* Washington, D.C.: the Association, 1962. A technical and factual report and projection of the problem of school finance in this decade.

Tiedt, Sidney W. *The Role of the Federal Government in Education.* New York: Oxford University Press, 1966. A concise analysis of historical background, arguments for and against Federal involvement in education, and present and future aspects of the problem.

7 Innovations in Education

Both professional and popular literature today are filled with descriptions and discussions of changes taking place in American education. Innovation seems to be the educational byword. Happy is the administrator, for instance, who can speak of the ungraded primary unit, computer-assisted instruction, team teaching, or independent study program being used in his school. There is no doubt that change is taking place, though, unfortunately, some innovations have almost become fads. Some schools have adopted a new form of organization, curriculum design, or instructional plan without thorough study and evaluation of and preparation for such a change. There should be more concern with the educational value of an innovation than with innovation itself.

Change is in the air, though change does not always imply progress. The schools of the 1970's will be different, but just how different remains to be seen. Enthusiastic projections have been made before, only to become so much wishful thinking. The educational enterprise is a conservative one, and ". . . the history of experimentation in American public education has for the most part been a story of failure. Such progress as has been made has taken place only at a glacial rate."[1] One recalls, for instance, the

[1] Robert H. Anderson, *Teaching in a World of Change* (New York: Harcourt, Brace & World, 1966), p. 4.

great predictions made for the educational use of radio or the fantastic transformation to be brought about by the use of educational films. Yet radio never has been widely used in the schools, nor has the full potential of the educational film as a learning device been realized. Dr. Conant, in his study of the comprehensive high school, expressed surprise at the limited use of television and programed learning he found in the schools.[2]

From among a number of educational innovations, three have been selected for discussion in this chapter: the nongraded school, team teaching, and programed learning and the teaching machine. These three were selected because they seem to be among those innovations that may affect the teacher of the 1970's to a considerable degree. Furthermore, they are innovations that have direct implications for *teaching,* the focus of this volume.

THE NONGRADED SCHOOL

The nongraded, or ungraded, plan is an attempt to overcome the rigidity and inflexibility of the graded school with its lock-step progress. In a graded system, the learners and what is to be learned are organized by grade. For example, generally all six-year-olds are placed in first grade and expected to master the first-grade curriculum before being "promoted" to the second grade. And so it goes on up the educational ladder. All students are expected to learn essentially the same thing at the same rate —it is assumed that if learners are all fed the same educational diet in similar amounts, all will become educationally healthy. Experience demonstrates that this just is not so. What is known today about the structure of knowledge and the way students learn renders ". . . obsolete and invalid the whole concept of expecting each child of a given age to conform to arbitrarily defined grade-level expectancies."[3]

Schools are organized in two ways—vertically and horizontally.

---

[2] James B. Conant. *The Comprehensive High School: A Second Report to Interested Citizens* (New York: McGraw-Hill Book Company, 1967), p. 70.
[3] Anderson, *op. cit.,* p. 46.

Vertical organization has to do with classifying students and determining their upward progress through the school; *horizontal* organization has to do with the way in which pupils are grouped for instruction and for allocation to teachers. The nongraded plan is a different way of organizing the school vertically—the series of levels found in the graded school (first grade, second grade, and so on) is replaced by a system that is based upon the individual learner and concern for his continuous progress. Major attention will be directed here to vertical school organization in discussing the nongraded plan; the question of grouping students for instruction will be considered in Chapter 9 in connection with the problem of providing instruction for the gifted student.

Vertical School Organization

Professor John I. Goodlad, a leader in the field of the nongraded school, describes three models of vertical school organization.[4] Model A is the typical graded school; Model C is the nongraded school; and Model B is a stage between the two using a multigrading or nongraded plan. A different conception of the function of the school or the role of individual differences is basic to each model. Advocates of Models A and B see the function of the school as imparting a specific body of subject matter. In the typical graded school, however, individual differences in students' ability and accomplishment are viewed as simply determining their chances of success in covering the designated subject matter; differences are not taken into account in the planning of the program or the organizational structure. Model B, on the other hand, takes individual differences into account in school organization so as to provide for different rates of progress.

Supporters of the nongraded school see the function of the school as that of developing the learner as an individual and as a member of society; such schools are learner-centered. Highly in-

----

[4] John I. Goodlad, *Planning and Organizing for Teaching.* Project on the Instructional Program of the Public Schools, National Education Association (Washington, D.C.: the Association, 1963), pp. 54–70.

dividualized programs are planned for students, and differences in many aspects of development are recognized. Pupils progress through the nongraded school at different rates, and there is variation in the kinds of programs offered to meet individual needs and abilities.

Progress in the graded school is regulated by nonpromotion—if a student does not master the curriculum of his grade he is not promoted to the next grade. This further emphasizes the focus on mastery of subject matter. While the same emphasis on subject matter prevails in Model B, nonpromotion is not used to regulate pupil progress through the school. Brighter students complete school more quickly, and slower students are allowed more years to complete their programs. In contrast to Models A and B, the emphasis in the nongraded school is on ways of knowing and thinking, not on the mastery of a specific body of subject matter.[5]

A *multigraded* plan may be used in Model B. Such a plan involves several grades in one class—grades 4, 5, and 6, for example. A particular child, therefore, could be in grade 5 for reading, grade 4 for social studies, and grade 3 for arithmetic. With such an arrangement, the teacher must provide for individual differences, and a child may move ahead in one area and lag behind in another.[6]

When a nongraded plan is used with Model B rather than a multigraded plan, it tends to be a levels approach, i.e., students are grouped not by grade but by levels of competency in a subject, usually reading. "Actually the levels plan of nongrading is akin to multigrading, with levels replacing grades."[7] Many ungraded primary plans, probably the most widely used nongraded arrangement, are levels plans. In the *ungraded primary* plan grades 1, 2, and 3 are done away with and a series of levels is established. Youngsters are free to move through the levels at their own rate. Thus, some children will complete the ungraded primary unit in two years, others will require four years, and the

[5] *Ibid.*, pp. 56–57.
[6] *Ibid.*, p. 62.
[7] *Ibid.*, p. 63.

majority will probably take the usual three years. However, there is still a common requirement for all, ". . . differentiation being provided in the rate of progression allowed."[8]

Model C, the truly nongraded school, has no set amount of subject matter to be "covered." There is a complete ignoring of grades.

> Students move forward through the school not as up a flight of steps but as along an incline. The sheer absence of grades is a reminder of the continuous progress desired. The rate of upward movement varies depending upon the readiness of the student to proceed.[9]

The "continuous progress" idea is basic to the nongraded plan. So also is the view that curriculum development is longitudinal and cannot be packaged for separate grades. Each youngster, when he has developed the necessary readiness, will go on to new learning appropriate for him. Therefore, for example, there is no "fourth grade," nor is there a "fourth-grade curriculum."

In a nongraded school, students still must be placed in classes, however. Professors Goodlad and Anderson recommend that overlapping class placements be used.[10] "Each nongraded class provides for a spread of several years in attainment from top to bottom child. In the nongraded plan, then, there are several alternative placements for each child at any time."[11] This provides for flexible pupil movement. A youngster may shift from one class to another, depending upon his need and stage of progress at the time.

The Dual Progress Plan

The Dual Progress Plan, developed by George Stoddard,[12] makes use of a form of nongradedness together with a modified

---

[8] *Ibid.*, p. 64.

[9] *Ibid.*, p. 68.

[10] John I. Goodlad and Robert H. Anderson, *The Nongraded Elementary School*, Revised edition (New York: Harcourt, Brace & World, 1963), p. 221.

[11] *Ibid.*, p. 223.

[12] George D. Stoddard, *The Dual Progress Plan* (New York: Harper and Brothers, 1961).

form of gradedness. It also embodies some other departures from the usual pattern of curriculum and instruction. Ossining and Long Beach in New York conducted a five-year cooperative study between 1958 and 1963. The plan has been introduced in about a dozen communities, usually in grades 4, 5, and 6.[13]

Under this plan, students spend about half of the school day with one teacher, a "home teacher," for instruction in language arts and social studies—the subjects called "cultural imperatives" by George Stoddard. These subjects are graded, and students must meet the grade standards in language arts and social studies in order to be promoted to the next grade. In this part of the day, physical education is also taught by a physical education specialist.

The "cultural electives" are taken up in the other half of the school day—these are subjects in which society will accept a wide range of competence. In these subjects—mathematics, science, art, and music—students are grouped on the basis of achievement and ability. Thus, in a science class there may be fourth, fifth, and sixth graders whose ability and achievement are presumably similar. Youngsters change classes here just as they do in high school.

This plan, in addition to providing a form of nongradedness, permits teachers to specialize at the elementary level. The Dual Progress Plan, however, has

> . . . failed of complete development, as have nongraded plans and team teaching, largely because of the magnitude of the curriculum problems (or opportunities) that it uncovers, because of administrative complexity, and because of the great difficulties involved in recruiting, training, and retraining teachers with the skills such programs require.[14]

Nongraded Secondary Schools

Much of what has been presented so far has been with refer-

[13] Anderson, *op. cit.*, p. 58.
[14] *Loc. cit.*

ence to the elementary school. There are nongraded secondary schools, though such schools represent less than 2 percent of all secondary schools, compared to an estimated 30 percent of elementary schools that are nongraded. Probably the best known nongraded high school is the one in Melbourne, Florida, near Cape Kennedy. The school's principal, B. Frank Brown, has defined a nongraded school as:

> . . . a place which makes arrangements for the individual student to pursue any course in which he is interested, and has the ability to achieve, without regard either to grade level or sequence.[15]

The program at Melbourne attempts to put this idea into practice. Grades, as such, are done away with, and students are grouped on the basis of the results obtained from nationally standardized achievement tests. Seven "phases" are used in setting up the school program:

Phase 1—Subjects are centered around remedial work.

Phase 2—Subjects are concerned with basic skills.

Phase 3—Subjects are designed for students seeking an average education.

Phase 4—Subjects are available for students desiring education in considerable depth.

Phase 5—Subjects are open to students who are willing to assume responsibility for their own learning and plan to go far beyond the boundaries of a single course.

Phase Q—Students whose creative talents are well developed in special areas should give consideration to this "Quest" phase of the curriculum. This is an important dimension of the phased organization designed to give thrust in the direction of individual fulfillment. In this phase a student may research an area in which he is deeply and broadly curious, either to develop creative powers or in quest of knowledge. A student may spend from one to three hours a day in Quest.

Phase X—Non-academic subjects which do not accommodate stu-

[15] B. Frank Brown, *The Nongraded High School* (Englewood Cliffs, N.J.: Prentice-Hall, 1963), p. 43.

dent mobility; e.g., typing, physical education. These subjects are ungraded but unphased.[16]

A student can be moved to a higher phase any time during the year if it becomes apparent that he has been assigned to a phase too low for him. Every attempt is made to permit students to work comfortably within their range of ability.

Obviously, the schedule at Melbourne is a complicated affair, for a particular student may be in Phase 3 in English, Phase 5 in American history, and so on for the balance of his schedule. But, since the student has "phase mobility" as well as continuing progress within each phase, he can move ahead as fast as his abilities will permit.

Problems of the Nongraded Plan

Any educational innovation is bound to present some problems. No doubt the reader has already sensed some of the problems of the nongraded plan. There is no real anti-nongraded literature as such, but Stuart Dean of the U.S. Office of Education has listed reasons why the nongraded school is considered undesirable by some educators.[17] Some of these reasons are that the nongraded plan lacks fixed standards and requirements; it places an impossible burden on the teacher; teachers are inadequately and insufficiently prepared for a nongraded program; its curriculum sequence is not specific or orderly; it does not guarantee improved teaching. There are other problems such as the extensive records required with the nongraded plan, the difficulty of getting parents to give up the "graded" notion, and the abuse of the term "nongraded." Many of these problems probably can be overcome with further experience in the use of the plan, but the problems do present real difficulties. As Professor Robert H. Anderson states:

. . . many of the seeming disadvantages of the nongraded school

[16] B. Frank Brown, "The Non-Graded High School," *Phi Delta Kappan*, Vol. 44, No. 5:206–209, February, 1963.

[17] Stuart E. Dean, "The Nongraded School: Is There Magic in It?" *School Life*, 47:22–23, December, 1964.

exist only because teachers and school officials have not yet developed the sophistication and flexibility that nongradedness demands. Only the curriculum-revision problems associated with nongradedness are of long-range importance and genuine severity.[18]

Currently, textbooks and other curriculum materials are on a graded basis. There is, for example, a fourth-grade science text, a fifth-grade science text, and so on for each grade. When a school shifts to a nongraded basis, few materials are readily available to meet the needs of the new vertical structure. If there were students, for instance, who ranged four or five grade levels in one class, one or two basic texts would not be sufficient. A number of books and materials at varying levels of difficulty would be required. Such a range of materials is not available, and the textbook publishers are not about to abandon the lucrative market of graded publications.

There are other aspects to the curriculum problems of the nongraded plan. For example:

> . . . which skill experiences are best arranged through individualized programs in which pupils can proceed at their own rates of speed, and which experiences are best reserved for groups? What topics, presented under what conditions, are appropriate for classes composed of youngsters whose academic potential and achievements range over a wide spectrum? What kinds of experiences can be shared by youngsters in multiage classes in which a great range of responses and contributions is possible?[19]

Such problems will need much study by curriculum experts before satisfactory solutions can be determined. Until these problems are solved, however, there is little hope that the nongraded school can make any real progress.

TEAM TEACHING

Team teaching is not actually a new idea in education, for

[18] Anderson, *Teaching in a World of Change*, p. 67.
[19] *Ibid.*, p. 50.

there have been attempts in the past to work out cooperative teaching arrangements and different organizational plans. The great amount of attention given to the idea during the last decade or so and the new forms of cooperative teaching developed, however, certainly qualify team teaching as an innovation. What is team teaching? How does it operate? What are its advantages and disadvantages? What will be its future? These are the questions to which attention will now be directed.

Team Teaching Defined

To define team teaching is not an easy task, because the term has been used to identify a variety of practices. As is the case with nongradedness and other newer educational plans and programs, the terms are used so loosely that they tend to have a less than precise meaning. One can observe "team teaching" at a particular school and find it quite different from "team teaching" at another school. There are, nevertheless, two general views of team teaching: it is seen by some as merely a new arrangement for instruction, while others view it as a new way of organizing the school horizontally. In a simple form, for example, some call "turn teaching" team teaching: one elementary teacher agrees to teach mathematics for another teacher if he will in turn teach social studies for the first teacher. An illustration of the more comprehensive view of team teaching would be that of Professors Goodlad and Anderson, who advocate the school be organized vertically as nongraded and horizontally on a team-teaching basis.[20]

Professor Anderson defines team teaching as follows:

> Team teaching is a formal type of cooperative staff organization in which a group of teachers, accepts the responsibility for planning, carrying out, and evaluating an educational program, or some major portion of a program, for an aggregate of pupils.[21]

[20] John I. Goodlad and Robert H. Anderson, *The Nongraded Elementary School.*

[21] Anderson, *Teaching in a World of Change,* p. 83. Original in italics.

Obviously, this definition involves a great deal more than two teachers exchanging classes. It involves a team of teachers cooperatively determining objectives and ways of reaching those objectives for a number of students. It involves cooperatively carrying out the formulated plans and evaluating how well the plans worked and how well the objectives were met. It involves more than two classes of children. It is a way of organizing teachers and students for learning.

In outlining an ideal arrangement for team teaching, Professor Anderson lists these points:

1. All team members (including children, wherever possible) participate in formulating broad overall objectives for the total program.
2. All team members participate at least weekly in formulating the more immediate objectives of the program.
3. All team members have an opportunity from time to time to contribute to the specific daily planning of their colleagues, and vice versa. That is to say, Miss Jones's lesson plan for Thursday afternoon is presented, discussed, and (it is hoped) modified for the better in Tuesday's team planning session, and, in turn, Miss Jones has equivalent opportunities to examine and improve the plans of her teammates.
4. Therefore, all team members are at all times at least conversant with the specific daily plans and professional repertoires of the other team members. As a result, it would be relatively easy for any team member to step into a colleague's teaching shoes in an emergency.
5. All team members at least occasionally (that is, several times a week) carry on teaching functions in the actual presence of colleagues who are either taking some part in the same lesson or simply sitting in as interested observers.
6. All team members participate periodically (weekly, if possible) in evaluation sessions of the overall as well as the current program.
7. And finally, each team member is the beneficiary of at least one weekly conference in which episodes of his own teaching (preferably those to which one or more colleagues were witnesses) are

carefully and objectively analyzed and out of which specific suggestions and ideas for professional improvements emanate.[22]

Teaching Teams in Action

The teaching team itself may be organized in several ways. It may, for example, be a group of teachers who are viewed as equals and who share responsibility and leadership functions. One will serve as leader, but without real authority over the others, or there may be a rotating leadership. Another type of organization, however, involves a hierarchy. There is a team leader who really has the responsibility and authority of leadership. Under him, there may be one or two senior teachers—master teachers. Below the master teachers would be the regular teachers. In the hierarchical plan, the team leader would perhaps be given $800 to $1,000 additional salary, and the senior teachers would receive some $300 to $500 above the salary level for the regular teachers. Paraprofessional aides may be used to assist in instructional and clerical tasks. The instructional assistants, perhaps teachers-in-training, could evaluate certain student work and handle instructional materials; the clerical aides could be used to relieve the team teachers from much of the routine clerical work.

Large- and small-group instruction and independent study are frequently used with team teaching, particularly at the secondary level. These practices are part of the Trump Plan, which advocates that students spend 40 percent of their time in large-group instruction, 20 percent of their time in small-group instruction, and the remaining 40 percent of their time in independent study.[23] The large groups consist of about 150 students; the small groups contain about 15 students.

There are problems with large-group instruction of course. Perhaps the principal one is that it tends to stress learning as merely the acquisition of facts if great emphasis is put on the use of lec-

---

[22] *Ibid.*, pp. 91–92.
[23] Lloyd Trump, *Images of the Future* (Urbana, Ill.: Commission on the Experimental Study of the Utilization of the Staff in the Secondary School, National Association of Secondary School Principals, a Department of the National Education Association, 1959), p. 9.

ture. It is also an impersonal method that does not allow for questioning by the students. What is more, poor teaching is only magnified by a large-group presentation. That is why only those who are skilled at working with large groups should participate in such instruction. Furthermore, existing schools do not always have sufficient number of rooms suitable for large groups.

On the other hand, large-group instruction can present outstanding teachers to more students. It can avoid duplication in the presentation of films or other visual aids, for the aid is used once for the large group, rather than for five or six smaller groups separately. If there is proper and immediate follow-up of the large-group presentation in the small groups, large-group instruction functions better. In these small groups—and it is important that they be kept *small*—questions can be raised by students and difficult points discussed further. The problem of existing facilities comes up, for many schools do not have a sufficient number of rooms suitable for small-group work. Through the installation of sliding partitions, however, larger rooms can be sectioned off into several smaller rooms for the small-group work.

Independent study is obviously something from which a good number of our students could profit. Able students and those with special interests could undertake independent projects or activities and perhaps gain a good deal more than they could from the regular class. (We all like to think that much learning is going on in our classes, but we surely realize that students do not have to be in class to learn.) And there are those who favor some independent study for all students. One wonders, however, about the value of such study for the less able student, for example, who needs much more direction in his study. Perhaps individualized instruction would have more value for him than would independent study.

Advantages and Disadvantages of Team Teaching

Many claims are made for team teaching and "glowing" reports of programs can be found in the literature. A real evaluation of team teaching cannot yet be given, however, for there is just not a sufficient amount of good research data available. Professors Fraenkel and Gross state, after referring to some of the studies of team teaching, that ". . . it is both misleading and dangerous to argue on the basis of research that any conclusive evidence of the effectiveness of team teaching has been established."[24] Hence, this discussion will have to be based upon the supposed assets and liabilities of the practice.

Team teaching gives teachers a chance to specialize. Thus, students can be offered a richer experience with specialists than they can in the usual self-contained classroom. By teaming teachers, many possibilities are presented for a variety of pupil groupings —large groups, small groups, individual instruction, groups with special needs. The team-teaching type of organization can make efficient use of facilities and resources. It can provide teachers with more time to plan and evaluate as well as relieve them of much routine through the use of instructional and clerical assistants. It can provide opportunities for stimulating the growth of teachers, and it can serve as a means of teacher training for both those preparing to teach and beginning teachers themselves. It can perhaps lead to newer and better approaches to curriculum and instruction.

Those who are more cautious about readily accepting team teaching point out that there are many teachers who could not or would not work well in this type of organization. Some teachers just do not care to work with others. Over the years, they have developed their own ways of doing things; they find it difficult to change. Of course, no teacher should be forced to work on a team if he really does not care to do so. But even some of those who do want to work in the team format may not have the necessary knowledge and skills to perform well. Yes, they can receive further training, which may help some greatly. There are, however, teachers who just do not have the ability or the personality to fit them for team teaching.

Human relations problems can become quite acute in team

[24] Jack R. Fraenkel and Richard E. Gross, "Team Teaching: A Note of Caution Is in Order," NEA Journal, 56:16, April, 1967.

teaching. Most teachers are not accustomed to being evaluated by their colleagues. It seems more than possible that some teachers would find it difficult to adjust to what could be continuous criticism by fellow teachers on the team. There is also the problem of the team leader who enjoys superior compensation and prestige. Granted that he may well deserve both of these extras, it still remains to be seen whether the majority of teachers will be "happy" with this arrangement.

Perhaps the most important question is whether student learning will benefit from team teaching more than from the usual classroom arrangement. Concerning this question, there is little research evidence to prove that students benefit more from team teaching. "Of the experiments which have been conducted, a large number indicate no significant differences in achievement between the experimental (team-taught) groups and the more traditional (self-contained with non-team teachers) groups."[25] Admittedly, there are built-in limitations in such studies. Improved performance as indicated by standardized achievement tests should not be the sole criterion by which to judge, for education is more than accumulating the factual knowledge measured by such tests. In addition to achievement test scores, other things would have to be determined, such as whether team teaching results in a better quality of thinking by students or an increase in the desire to learn.

Earlier some problems of large-group instruction and inadequate facilities were discussed in relation to team teaching. The problem of administrative support must also be mentioned. Unless the administration is committed to making the kinds of changes and accommodations necessary for team teaching, it is doubtful that the project will be successful. Without being given sufficient time for planning, for example, faculty members will be hard pressed to function well in a team-teaching format.

This discussion has perhaps dealt more with the problems related to team teaching than with its probable benefits. The intention was not to depreciate the possible future value of this inno-

[25] *Loc. cit.*

vation, for it may have much to offer education. It is simply that
". . . team teaching at this stage can only be regarded as primitive
and that theories and procedures must be further developed before the long-range usefulness and applicability of team teaching
can be adequately evaluated."[26]

PROGRAMED LEARNING AND TEACHING MACHINES

Programed learning, or programed instruction, stems from research on the learning process carried on over quite a period of
years. The programed-instruction movement, however, began
about 1954 with the work of the noted educational psychologist
Professor B. F. Skinner of Harvard University. Teaching machines are merely devices for presenting programed material; it is
not necessary to use teaching machines in order to have programed instruction.

What Is Programed Learning?

Programed learning is not just an aid to learning; it is a way of
learning. The material to be learned is *programed*—it is broken
down into a series of small, discrete steps known as *frames*. Each
frame is presented to the learner and contains some information
(the stimulus), a question to be answered (the response), and
the correct answer against which the student may check his
answer (the confirmation). There are basically two methods of
programing: *linear* programing and *branching* or intrinsic programing.

Linear programing is based upon what Skinner calls *operant
conditioning*, i.e., ". . . a process whereby animal or human subjects are stimulated to behave toward predetermined goals
through a series of small actions and consequent reinforce-
ments."[27] The information in the frame is the stimulus to which
the learner responds. The learner then receives instant feedback

[26] Anderson, *Teaching in a World of Change*, p. 101.
[27] W. Lee Garner, *Programed Instruction*, The Library of Education (New
York: The Center for Applied Research in Education, Inc., 1966), p. 9.

as to whether his response is correct or not. The immediate feedback is important, for it is known that the more immediate the confirmation, or reinforcement, the better an individual learns. This is also true if the student's response is incorrect, because his error is immediately corrected.

In the operant-conditioning kind of program, the emphasis is on the response—a written word or phrase placed by the learner in the blank provided. The learner proceeds sequentially from frame to frame through the program as the material progresses from the rather simple to the more complex. Answers are given in the next frame so as to discourage cheating.

Branching programs make use of multiple-choice questions which are diagnostic in nature and are used to check periodically on student progress. The questions are placed throughout conventional prose material and each step is determined by the answer to the previous question. If his response is correct, the student goes on to more advanced material; if his response is incorrect, it will be corrected by the next frame, and he will then be sent off on a branch of remedial frames. These remedial frames will ensure his understanding of the previous material before the student is returned to the main line of the program. Thus, branching programs do allow for differences in learner response, while linear programs provide a fixed sequence of items. Through extensive pretesting to determine the learner's background, though, various points of entry in the linear program can be used to allow for differences in learners.

The *scrambled book* is a branching program set in book form. The learner does not proceed through the pages consecutively however. Material and a diagnostic question are presented. Depending upon which of the multiple choices the learner selects, he is referred to a different page in the book. Since the pages have been randomly scrambled, clues to the correct answer are not given by the page numbers. Ultimately, all crucial information is covered by the learners, though each learner may have taken a slightly different path through the various branches to the end.

Teaching Machines

Teaching machines, as was pointed out above, are not necessary in order to make use of programed materials. They are no more than devices for presenting programs, but they can vary from very simple (paper boxes with wind-up knobs) to very complex types (computer-based systems). As early as 1925 psychologist Sidney Pressey developed a simple teaching machine that was operated by a hand crank, but the modern teaching machine was pioneered by Professor Skinner. A simple type of teaching machine would present a question in a window to be answered by the student who records his answer on a roll of paper inside the machine. In another version, he would punch a key that would record his answer on tape. The student then operates a crank that moves his answer out of the window so that he cannot change it and presents him with the correct answer. The student's answers are then permanently recorded and scored. Unlike homework or tests, which may not be returned for days, immediate results are given. Thus, learning is immediately reinforced.

A more complicated type of teaching machine involves a television screen on which a student is shown a scene or some sort of problem. Questions are posed by the machine, and the student responds by punching a keyboard that is wired into an electronic computer. Though it seems Orwellian, the computer tells him whether he is "right" or "wrong"; if wrong, the student may push a button marked "help" and the computer will decide what kind of additional information he will need to solve the problem. After sufficient review of the remedial material presented by the machine, the student may push an "aha" button, at which time the computer returns him to the main line of questions and answers. This illustration of computer-assisted instruction (CAI) indicates the fantastic possibilities inherent in the application of programed instruction to computer systems.

Pros and Cons of Programed Learning

There are a number of advantages claimed for programed

learning. Proponents stress that individual differences can be met better through programed instruction. Students can move at their own rate through programed materials; branching programs can provide review for those having difficulty with the material; programs with varying levels of difficulty can be used for learners of varying levels of ability. Furthermore, programed learning can be used for independent study, an ingredient in other innovations such as team teaching and nongradedness. Courses not otherwise available, particularly in the small high school, can be offered through programed learning. Surely it is to be preferred to instruction by an unprepared and unqualified teacher in advanced courses. Students can take home programed textbooks and certain inexpensive teaching machines, and the teacher need not worry that students will learn wrong responses as they frequently do with ordinary homework.

Programed learning can relieve teachers of much drudgery and routine in presenting and reviewing material and in correcting tests and homework. Teachers are then freed to work with individual students and to pursue the more creative aspects of teaching. More knowledge can be secured about human learning because programing focuses attention on the dynamics of human understanding and on the very process by which people learn, as discussed in Chapter 3. The promise is even held out that all learners can achieve mastery at every stage of presentation with programed instruction.

Many educators are cautious and some are quite concerned about the prospects of programed learning. Some schools have "got on the bandwagon" and adopted programed materials that were of poor quality and teaching machines of questionable value. This did not help programed instruction get off to a good start. The promise that every student would achieve mastery at the end of a program has yet to be realized.[28] Programed learning is in essence a series of questions and answers, and teachers and laymen must not come to expect more from it than it is capable of

[28] Garner, *op. cit.*, p. 40.

doing. To rely on programed learning as the sole means of instruction would be most unwise, for the purposes of education, as discussed in Chapter 3, go beyond simply imparting knowledge. No machine or program can completely take the place of the teacher. With increased use of technology in education, the role of the teacher will probably change. But as pointed out in Chapter 1, there will always be an important place for the human element in teaching.

From the standpoint of theory, there are many who question the kind of learning developed through Skinner's operant conditioning. It is but one kind of learning. For example, there is evidence to show that some kinds of learning occur quite effectively when the whole is first taken into perspective and the parts are then analyzed as components in relation to the whole. What also of man's powers of imagination and creativeness and his capacity to dissent? Caution must be exercised that in programing overemphasis is not placed upon conformity. Garner points out that more attention must be paid to values in programing:

> Students can get a notion that learning is always a process of tracking an easily followed sequence of fragmentary units, and that information and concepts will always be ready-made for their consumption. If they are protected from complexity, they will be unadjusted to the fact that the life they will be leading will be anything but neatly arranged or simplistic.[29]

There is disagreement among authorities about the method of programing to be used. Sidney L. Pressey has questioned the use of the linear program format. In discussing such a format in relation to the typical textbook, Pressey states:

> As a way to present matter to be learned, the average textbook may not be best. But thousands of frames on a teaching-machine roll or strung through a programed book would seem close to the worst. To make a very bad pun, the programers have "framed" the text-

[29] *Ibid.*, p. 97.

book. Instead of trying to improve their programs, they might better consider very broadly how best to present matter for learning. The opinion is ventured that the best will be found closer to texts than to their programs.[30]

There has been a moving away from the strictly linear sequence toward multiple paths with larger step sizes, and more attempts are being made to adapt to the individual learner's needs.[31] Perhaps in the future programed learning will come to fill all that it promises for education. But for now, more research is needed, and more knowledge needs to be given teachers and administrators about the true value and appropriate place of programed learning in American education.

SUGGESTED ACTIVITIES

1. Arrange with your instructor, if possible, to visit a school making use of some form of nongradedness, team teaching, or programed learning.
2. Prepare a written report on some educational innovation not discussed in this chapter such as instructional television or the use of computers in education.
3. Form a committee to investigate and report to the class about the ways in which educational television is now being used in your state as well as proposals for its future use.
4. Secure literature from several of the companies marketing programed materials and teaching machines and present a report to the class in which you discuss the kinds of materials and machines available, their prices (if available), and their advertised merits.
5. Invite an audiovisual specialist to speak to the class about recent developments in his field.
6. Interview several experienced teachers about their attitudes toward current educational innovations and compare their responses with

[30] Sidney L. Pressey, "Teaching Machine (and Learning Theory) Crises," Stan Dropkin, Harold Full, and Ernest Schwarz, eds., *Contemporary American Education: An Anthology of Issues, Problems, Challenges* (New York: The Macmillan Company, 1965), p. 404.

[31] Garner, *op. cit.*, p. 33.

those you secure from several beginning teachers. What similarities
or differences do you find in the two sets of responses?

7. Plan with your instructor and audiovisual department to arrange a
demonstration of sample programed materials and teaching machines for the class.

SELECTED REFERENCES

Anderson, Robert H. *Teaching in a World of Change.* New York: Harcourt, Brace & World, 1966. An examination of the context within
which the modern teacher works with emphasis on change. Chapters
are devoted to team teaching, the nongraded school, and the library-
centered school.

Bair, Medill, and Woodward, Richard G. *Team Teaching in Action.*
Boston: Houghton Mifflin Co., 1964. Intended more for the practic-
ing teacher, this book draws on the authors' experience in the Lex-
ington (Mass.) teaching-team project.

Beggs, David W., ed. *Team Teaching: Bold New Venture.* Indianapolis, Ind.: Unified College Press, 1964. An analysis of various aspects
of team teaching is given by twelve authors.

Brown, B. Frank. *The Nongraded High School.* Englewood Cliffs,
N.J.: Prentice-Hall, 1963. Describes the institution of the nongraded
program at Melbourne High School in Florida; presents the advantages of such a program over the traditional graded program.

DeCecco, John P. *Educational Technology: Readings in Programed Instruction.* New York: Holt, Rinehart and Winston, 1964. Presents a
comprehensive view on all areas of programed instruction.

Garner, W. Lee. *Programed Instruction.* The Library of Education.
New York: The Center for Applied Research in Education, 1966. An
introduction to programed instruction. See particularly Chapter II,
"Basic Theories, Principles and Techniques," and Chapter III, "Programed Instruction in Education."

Gerard, R. W., ed. *Computers and Education.* New York: McGraw-
Hill Book Company, 1967. This authoritative source derives from a
conference held at the University of California at Irvine on the future of computers and education. See especially Sessions I and II on
the learning and technical aspects of computer-assisted instruction
(CAI).

Goodlad, John I., and Anderson, Robert H. *The Nongraded Elementary School.* Revised edition. New York: Harcourt, Brace & World, 1963. A leading work which explores the ideas and philosophy as well as the organization and operation of the nongraded school.

Goodlad, John I. *Planning and Organizing for Teaching.* Project on the Instructional Program of the Public Schools, National Education Association. Washington, D.C.: the Association, 1963. Deals with problems of curriculum, school, and classroom organization; identifies major issues; and makes recommendations. See especially Chapter Three, "Toward Improved School Organization."

Lange, Phil C., ed. *Programmed Instruction.* Sixty-sixth Yearbook of the National Society for the Study of Education, Part II. Chicago: The University of Chicago Press, 1967. A survey of the historical and psychological foundations of programed instruction. Present methods are evaluated, and probable developments are projected.

Miller, Richard I., ed. *Perspectives on Educational Change.* New York: Appleton-Century-Crofts Division of Meredith Publishing Company, 1967. Focuses on the process of educational change, which is considered in both general and specific terms.

Phi Delta Kappan. "Programed Instruction," 44:241–302, March, 1963. Sixteen articles by leaders in the field of programed instruction in this special issue. Deals with both theoretical and practical problems.

Shaplin, Judson T., and Olds, Henry F., Jr., eds. *Team Teaching.* New York: Harper & Row, Publishers, 1964. A definitive and scholarly treatment of the topic by the editors and contributors.

Skinner, Burrhus F. "Reflections on a Decade of Teaching Machines," *Teachers College Record,* 65:168–177, November, 1963. Discusses the significance of the teaching-machine movement in education and of programed learning in the new pedagogy.

Trow, William Clark. *Teacher and Technology: New Designs for Learning.* New York: Appleton-Century-Crofts, 1963. A paperback on technological change in the schools. Includes a consideration of television and programed learning.

Trump, J. Lloyd, and Baynham, Dorsey. *Focus on Change: Guide to Better Schools.* Chicago: Rand McNally & Co., 1961. A report by the Commission on the Experimental Study of the Utilization of the Staff in Secondary School, appointed by the National Association of

Secondary School Principals, NEA. The "Trump Plan" involves team teaching, large- and small-group instruction, and independent study.

8 Careers in Education

There are many careers one could pursue within the broad field of education. Whole volumes are devoted to such careers. In this chapter, the author has selected for discussion six rather specialized teaching areas probably not so familiar to the reader: art education, business education, industrial arts education, music education, physical education for women, and speech therapy. These areas were selected not only because of their unfamiliarity as careers, but also because they represent parts of the program of public education that may not be very well understood. For similar reasons the work of three specialists in the area of pupil personnel services will be considered: the school counselor, the school psychologist, and the school social worker. And, because a number of teachers move into administration, that area of careers will also be included. The various areas will be taken up in alphabetical order; ample materials for further investigation will be found in the listed references at the end of this chapter.

ADMINISTRATION

A number of opportunities are available in public school administration for those with initiative, leadership, and experience. The positions to be discussed here are superintendent, assistant superintendent, principal, and assistant principal. There are a number of other administrative positions, however, that will not be included in this discussion, like department heads, already discussed in Chapter 4; directors of specific areas or fields such as elementary education or physical education; positions concerned with the business management of the school district and the supervision of buildings and grounds.

School Superintendent[1]

While the superintendent holds the best-paying position in the public schools,[2] his position is also the most difficult and demanding one. The demands and difficulties of his work are apparent in the four principal parts of his job:

1. *Improving educational opportunity.* All aspects of the instructional program are included in this part; such questions as what shall be taught and how it shall be taught are considered here.
2. *Obtaining and developing personnel.* The divisions of the job concerned with recruitment, selection, placement, and promotion of personnel are relevant here. All matters of personnel administration are likewise considered. Pupil personnel problems are considered under this head in addition to matters relating to professional and non-professional personnel.
3. *Maintaining effective relations with the community.* This part of the job is more broadly conceived than mere public relations. It includes interpreting the schools to the public and studying the community so as to further education.
4. *Providing and maintaining funds and facilities.* The business and housekeeping aspects of school administration are included in this part of the job. Included are budget planning, plant maintenance, construction and renovation of buildings, and similar functions.[3]

[1] Reference in this discussion is to the local superintendent of schools in a school district with a student population of about 20,000.

[2] In systems with enrollments of 25,000 or more, the average maximum salary paid to superintendents was $26,017 in 1966–67; with 6,000–11,999 enrollment, it was $19,387. (National Education Association, Research Division, *Salary Schedules for Administrative Personnel, 1966–67,* Public-School Salaries Series, Research Report 1967-R3 [Washington, D.C.: the Association, 1967], p. 5.)

[3] Daniel E. Griffiths, *The School Superintendent,* The Library of Education (New York: The Center for Applied Research in Education, 1966), pp. 70–71.

Attempting to improve educational opportunity has become a major responsibility as schools enroll more and more young people and attempt to do more and more for them. Now there is concern for nursery school, junior college, and adult education. In short, the superintendent needs to be concerned about educational opportunity for all within his school district.

The superintendent needs assistance in meeting his responsibilities. In arriving at aims and objectives of the schools, for instance, he may utilize a committee composed of teachers, administrators, and lay citizens. He cannot spend his time working directly on the actual improvement of instruction, so these responsibilities are turned over to building principals, supervisors, and consultants. Such activities as construction of student schedules, the keeping of pupil personnel records, and numerous technical functions are turned over to others.[4]

Recruiting, selecting, placing, promoting, and training personnel is a major responsibility of the superintendent as is developing and maintaining high morale among the staff. He needs to establish a sound organization structure and a grievance system. Many personnel problems in today's schools are due partly to faulty organizational structure and the lack of a mechanism by which grievances can be communicated to the administration and the board of education. This need for effective communication is also evident in interpreting the schools to the community. A plan of public relations needs to be developed, and such a plan must provide for two-way communication. Educational needs and the work of the schools must be presented, and the opinions, attitudes, and feelings of the community must be assessed. The community must be involved in the schools if the school system is to be adequately provided with funds and facilities. The function of providing funds and facilities requires much of the time and skill of the superintendent, for preparation of the school budget and the development of long-range plans for the school district are his responsibilities.[5]

[4] *Ibid.*, pp. 72–74.
[5] *Ibid.*, pp. 75–79.

It is obvious that the superintendent must be a man of many talents in order to perform effectively and efficiently in all aspects of his work. He must have a deep and broad knowledge of education; he must be able to make sound judgments; he must know and understand human behavior of individuals and groups; and he must have courage and vision. And this is only a partial list of desirable characteristics. It is not surprising then that the American Association of School Administrators recommends at least two years of graduate study in the education of superintendents.[6] Teaching experience, of course, is required for the superintendency. In large school districts, the pattern for reaching the position is usually teacher, principal, assistant or associate superintendent, superintendent. In small communities, the common pattern is teacher, principal, superintendent.[7]

Assistant Superintendent

The principal function of the assistant superintendent is to aid the superintendent who, in a large district, cannot handle all of the responsibilities by himself. There may, in fact, be assistant superintendents in charge of personnel administration, curriculum, public relations, and business management. Or there may be but one assistant superintendent who takes on such duties as the superintendent may designate. As noted above, assistant superintendents usually come from the ranks of principals and can move on to the superintendency. The position of assistant superintendent is an excellent training ground not only for the superintendency but for other educational positions such as those at the county or state level.

Principal

Principals constitute both the largest group of administrators and the most visible one, for they head the individual school—the

[6] American Association of School Administrators, *Professional Administrators for America's Schools,* Thirty-Eighth Yearbook (Washington, D.C.: the Association, 1960), p. 177.
[7] Griffiths, *op. cit.,* p. 48.

unit of education best known to students, parents, and the general public. Teaching principals are found in small schools where their duties include teaching as well as administration. When a principal is in charge of both elementary and secondary schools, he is usually known as a supervising principal. Assistant principals are normally found in large school districts.

A master's degree and successful teaching experience are generally required for the position of principal. Salaries earned are better than those for teachers. For instance, in districts with enrollment of 25,000 or more students in 1966–67, the average salary for senior high school principals was $10,918; for junior high school principals, it was $10,155; and for elementary school principals, it was $9,191.[8] The estimated average salary for elementary teachers in 1966–67, on the other hand, was $6,069; for secondary teachers, the comparable figure was $7,095.[9]

The principal has a multitude of things to do. Ideally, he is responsible for the total educational program of the school and the management of the school's affairs. He is, therefore, concerned with instruction and curriculum. He may take part in the selection of new staff members, the orientation of new teachers, and the further development of the staff's capabilities. The principal will supervise the work of the teachers, the maintenance staff, and perhaps a cafeteria staff. And he must be concerned with textbooks, equipment, and supplies. There is much paper work to be done: correspondence, reports, bulletins, and memorandums. There are many meetings with the superintendent, other administrators, the school staff, parents, and community groups to attend. The principal must be concerned with proper pupil behavior, a system of reporting pupil progress to parents, and the health and safety of all in the school. In addition to an active interest in student affairs, the principal must take an active role in community affairs.

[8] National Education Association, Research Division, *Salary Schedules for Administrative Personnel,* Public School Salaries Series, Research Report 1967-R3 (Washington, D.C.: the Association, 1967), p. 10.
[9] National Education Association, Research Division, *Rankings of the States,* Research Report 1967-R1 (Washington, D.C.: the Association, 1967), p. 26.

Throughout his work, the principal must deal with a variety of groups, many of which will make different demands on him. He is the "man in the middle" because he stands between the central administration and the teaching staff. He must carry out school district policies while meeting the professional and personal needs of the teaching staff. This often can bring about conflict, for policy and teacher needs are not always identical. While the central administration and the teachers may have different expectations for the principal, the community may well have expectations different from both groups. Furthermore, the principal's professional organizations may set expectations conflicting with all of the above groups.[10]

Assistant Principal

Some large elementary schools have assistant principals, but the position is much more common in the secondary school where the title used is frequently "vice-principal." Obviously, the assistant principal "assists" the principal, but the way in which he assists varies. It is the principal's responsibility to define the role of the assistant principal.[11] The principal, however, should delegate authority commensurate with the responsibilities given the assistant principal. Making someone responsible for a particular function without giving him the necessary authority is a poor administrative practice.

In a particular secondary school there may be one or more assistant principals to administer and/or supervise any or all of the following: counseling and guidance, attendance, club programs, student assemblies, school calendar, cafeteria, curriculum improvement, student teachers, and instructional materials. When the principal is absent, the vice-principal is in charge of the school. A position with duties such as the above provides an ex-

[10] Daniel E. Griffiths in the introduction to Samuel Goldman, *The School Principal*, The Library of Education (New York: The Center for Applied Research in Education, 1966), p. vii.

[11] Gareth B. Goddard, "The Assistant Principal—Understudy or Partner in Professional Leadership," *National Association of Secondary School Principals Bulletin*, 46, No. 275:33, September, 1962.

cellent opportunity for acquiring the necessary knowledge and experience that help to prepare one for the principalship.

ART EDUCATION

Art education opportunities in the public schools consist of such positions as art specialist for the elementary school, secondary teacher of art, department head, and art education supervisor. The art teacher should possess the qualities found in any good teacher, to be sure. Beyond these qualities, however, every art teacher, ideally, should be an active creative artist.[12] Such creative activity can deepen the teacher's understanding of the work his pupils are doing. Certainly, then, if one is considering art education as a career, he should have artistic talent and be interested in pursuing the cultivation of that talent.

The position of art specialist for the elementary school is singled out for attention here because the reader may be less familiar with this position. Furthermore, it is felt that in such work the art teacher can exert a great influence upon developing the expressive capacity of children and educating them to create and respond to art.

Art education in the elementary school is not just "fun" or "play." "Art experience provides opportunity for heightening sensitivity to the physical world, introducing order into sense impressions, and bringing into existence a visible token of imagination and feeling."[13] This kind of art experience is not found in simply tracing, copying, or in other ways producing just what the teacher wants. Such experience brings about mere compliance on the part of children and certainly does not foster creativity. What kinds of things would one find in a good elementary school art program?

The current art program employs a wide variety of materials and procedures. It makes use of both three-dimensional techniques, such

[12] Hilda Present Lewis, *Art Education in the Elementary School* (Washington, D.C.: National Education Association, 1961), p. 29.
[13] *Ibid.*, p. 3.

as papier mâché, clay modeling, and wood construction, and two-dimensional techniques, such as drawing, painting, printing, and finger painting. It includes abstract and representational art, group and individual projects, and the production of both functional and purely ornamental objects.[14]

These materials and procedures, together with a good art teacher, can make for a fine program.

The art specialist in the elementary school might be an itinerant teacher going to several elementary schools to actually teach art to boys and girls. Or she could be serving as a consultant on call to assist the elementary teachers in planning art activities. In the latter position the art teacher may, for example, conduct workshops for the elementary teachers in anticipation of appropriate art activities for an up-coming holiday observance or special event. In an ideal situation, the art consultant would work with a classroom teacher in devising art activities to coordinate with a unit of study she was planning. The teacher would plan with the specialist art activities that could be integrated in the unit of study to make the learning more interesting and valuable for the students.

For someone who has the artistic ability, the qualities of a good teacher, and the necessary skill in interpersonal relations a career in art education offers a great challenge and much satisfaction.

BUSINESS EDUCATION

The teacher of business education at the secondary level is concerned with both general and vocational education. Business education contributes to general education (education that has value for all students), for it helps the student to become a more intelligent consumer of goods and services; it also increases the student's proficiency to function well in the economic aspects of our society. Courses like business arithmetic, general business, ad-

[14] *Ibid.*, p. 3.

vertising, and business law can deal with knowledge and skills of value to all students. Examples of such knowledge and skills are how to borrow money intelligently; how to compute interest and discount; how to manage a checking account; how to complete income tax forms; what constitutes a legal contract; what kind of life insurance to buy; and how to detect false or misleading advertisements.

The vocational aspect of business education (preparing students for entry into the world of work) has always been of importance. This aspect has been given increased emphasis in recent years, however, particularly with the passage of the Vocational Education Act of 1963. This is the first Act to include business and office occupations in federally aided programs. Typewriting, shorthand, bookkeeping, clerical practice, office machines, and other business courses help the student to gain the knowledge, skills, understandings, and attitudes necessary for securing initial employment. Typewriting, which is also a useful general skill, has the largest enrollment of any business subject in the secondary curriculum, 23 percent of high school students.[15]

The business education teacher should have a good collegiate preparation for teaching which includes a concentration on mastery of a variety of business subjects.[16] While some states have only one certificate for business education requiring the candidate to be competent in all business areas, other states grant several certificates, perhaps one for the secretarial area, one for bookkeeping and accounting, and one for general business or social business. Whether business experience is required or not, the prospective teacher of business subjects should have such experience.[17] Furthermore, it is desirable for the business teacher

[15] U.S. Department of Health, Education and Welfare, *Summary of Offerings and Enrollments in High School Subjects, 1960–1961* (Washington, D.C.: U.S. Government Printing Office, July, 1964), p. 2.

[16] Frank M. Herndon, "A Career in Teaching the Business Subjects," *Business Education Forum*, 18:9, January, 1964.

[17] Lloyd V. Douglas, James T. Blanford, and Ruth I. Anderson, *Teaching Business Subjects*, Second edition (Englewood Cliffs, N.J.: Prentice-Hall, 1965), p. 11.

to renew this work experience from time to time in order to keep current with the business world.

Ideally, business education should be an important area of the secondary school program. Too often, it is not. This is due to a number of things. In some schools, business courses have been used by administrators as "dumping grounds" for students who were behavior problems or who could not show satisfactory achievement in other parts of the program.[18] This has tended to give business education, its teachers, and its students "second-class citizenship" in the high school. Another contributing factor has been the inability of college-bound students to fit business courses into their crowded programs, should they be interested in such courses. Some business teachers themselves have not enhanced the position of business education because of their limited view of the field and their work in it. They do not see business education in its broader socio-economic aspects; they see themselves simply as teachers of some basic business skills.

The author certainly does not wish to discourage anyone from considering business education as a teaching career, but he does wish to point out what has sometimes been the "reality" for the business teacher. There is a need for able young people to come into the field. There is now and will continue to be for some time a shortage of well-qualified business teachers.[19] Furthermore, the opportunities for the teacher of business education at the post-secondary level are expanding as the number of community colleges continues to increase.

INDUSTRIAL ARTS

Industrial arts education, as general education, is concerned with a study of our industrial society through laboratory-class-

---

[18] Unfortunately, the same situation often prevails for art courses and other so-called nonacademic courses.

[19] C. A. Nolan, Carlos K. Hayden, and Dean R. Malsbary, *Principles and Problems of Business Education,* Third edition (Cincinnati: South-Western Publishing Company, 1967), p. 51.

room experiences. The role of industry and technology is viewed in the study of the

> . . . history, growth, and development of industrial organizations, materials, products, processes and related problems. . . . It provides experiences in developing basic skills and knowledge common to many occupations and professions.[20]

Industrial arts is usually a required subject in the junior high school and is offered as an aspect of general education. Students are introduced to various areas of industry and may study natural and synthetic materials, production methods, and the resulting products. Industrial and technological problems are also explored.

In the senior high school, industrial arts is generally offered on an elective basis. The courses become more technical and specialized and may include subjects such as the following: automotives, ceramics, design, drawing, electricity-electronics, graphic arts, metalworking, plastics, textiles, and woodworking. Though most industrial arts educators do not agree with him, Dr. Conant believes that these courses should develop skills that are marketable, i.e., they should prepare the student for a job and not simply give him a practical acquaintance with the industrial world.[21] This requires a teacher who is both qualified and vocationally oriented.

> It must be remembered by the teacher that the students are being trained to get a skilled job and hold it in a competitive world. Not only must the teacher be qualified for the purpose, but the tools must be qualified too.[22]

Trade and industrial education should provide knowledge of good workmanship and design; skill in the use of the tools and

---

[20] American Industrial Arts Association, *A Career in Teaching Industrial Arts* (Washington, D.C.: the Association, n.d.).

[21] James B. Conant, *Slums and Suburbs* (New York: McGraw-Hill Book Company, 1961), p. 107.

[22] The Institute for Research, *Trade and Vocational Teaching as a Career*, Research Number 231 (Chicago: the Institute, 1966), p. 14.

machines of production; good work habits and appreciation of efficiency; resourcefulness, self-reliance, and self-discipline; and the ability to work well with others.[23]

While certification requirements vary, the prospective industrial arts teacher should have completed his bachelor's degree in an accredited college with a good program of industrial arts education. Actual experience in industry is a must, if the teacher is to be really well prepared. Furthermore, he needs to be creative and imaginative, to truly enjoy working with students, and to possess organizational abilities. Patience and calmness of disposition are also important, particularly for his work with individuals and small groups who are at the beginning stages of learning.

There is a pronounced need for industrial arts teachers and the opportunities in the field are good.

MUSIC EDUCATION

Music education in the public schools offers positions in teaching at the elementary or secondary level as well as in supervision of the music program. Music education is similar to art education in that in addition to the usual requirements for teaching one needs a special talent—in this case, musical talent. Not only talent and a liking for music are necessary, but also the desire to assist others in sharing in the beauty, joy, and satisfaction of music. The prospective music educator must be willing to develop his talent further so that he has capacity in both vocal and instrumental music. The Music Educators National Conference also recommends functional facility in piano for all music teachers.[24]

The opportunities in music education are good. The field of music education is so broad today that a capable teacher can generally secure a position that enables him to spend his time work-

[23] E. Dale Davis, *Focus on Secondary Education: An Introduction to Principles and Practices* (Glenview, Ill.: Scott Foresman and Company, 1966), p. 146.

[24] Music Educators National Conference, *A Career in Music Education* (Washington, D.C.: Music Educators National Conference, National Education Association, 1965), p. 11.

ing with the phase of music that interests him most.[25] He may find that instrumental music interests him most and wish to work with this phase of music. On the other hand, he may want to help others become intelligent appreciators of music and thus work more in a classroom situation with general music. Or he may find that he would like to do several of these things. The music program, though, is not a standardized one and ". . . the teacher's duties in one community can be quite different from those in another."[26]

A good collegiate program of preparation for music teaching will provide experience in all areas of music. Proficiency in vocal and instrumental music will be developed, and opportunities will be afforded in conducting. There will be other music courses such as composition, arranging, harmony, and sight singing. All of this, of course, is in addition to work in general education and professional education.

When the new teacher becomes certified, he may decide to seek a position in elementary school music. Here he may be the special music teacher who actually teaches music to the boys and girls; or he may be the music consultant who assists the classroom teacher in planning her music program; or he may be an instrumental specialist who gives instrumental lessons and conducts the band or orchestra if the school has one.

In the junior high school and the senior high school, the music teacher may do a variety of things or may specialize. There are general and special music classes as well as instrumental and vocal performing groups. The program will vary with the size of the school. As a matter of fact, in a small school district the music teacher may teach at both the elementary and secondary level. In any event, he will work with individuals and with large and small groups.

It would be fair to say that in a number of school systems music education is not well supported. This is partly due to the

[25] *Ibid.*, p. 7.
[26] Ira C. Singleton, *Music in Secondary Schools* (Boston: Allyn and Bacon, 1963), p. 3.

cost of a good program, but it is also due to the fact that the purpose of music education is not fully understood. To many, unfortunately, it is just a frill or "fun" and not considered an important part of the curriculum. More needs to be done to help some educators and part of the public to realize the value of music—not only its cultural value, but the good sense of aural beauty it can develop, the creative experience it can provide, and the life-long interest or recreation it can become.

PHYSICAL EDUCATION FOR WOMEN

While there is an oversupply of men in physical education, there is a shortage of women in the field. Hence, the opportunities in physical education for women are excellent. This is especially true in the elementary school where there is growing recognition that physical education specialists are needed, particularly in grades 4, 5, and 6.[27] Therefore, attention here is directed to the career possibilities for women in elementary school physical education.

A good physical education program in the elementary school is based upon a thorough knowledge of how physical education can contribute to the overall growth and development of children at each age level. However, too many elementary schools have poor programs or no real program at all:

All too often elementary school physical education is a haphazard affair in which the teacher supervises the choosing of sides or the assembling in formation for playing a game, which has been endorsed as a favorite by the youngsters, and then stands on the sidelines until the ringing of the bell signifies the end of the physical education period. Obviously, while such an activity may be "physical," it is not "education" to any significant degree.[28]

The physical education period should provide systematic learning

[27] Charles A. Bucher, *Foundations of Physical Education,* Fourth edition (St. Louis: The C. V. Mosby Company, 1964), pp. 553–554.
[28] Hollis F. Fait, *Physical Education for the Elementary School Child* (Philadelphia: W. B. Saunders Company, 1964), p. 3.

experiences and is different from recess or after-school play. However, it is not possible to give boys and girls all of the activity they need in one period, since most children should have between three to five hours of vigorous physical exercise each day.[29]

The physical education program is concerned with developing good physical fitness, motor skills and coordination, sound attitudes, and knowledge. "Fair play" and "good sportsmanship," taking turns, and abiding by the rules can be learned. Also, the role of play in transmitting the culture has been widely recognized.[30] Many forms of human movement are involved in the program: ". . . games and sports, rhythms and dance, and such exercises as gymnastics, apparatus, stunts, and tumbling."[31] In view of the increasing amount of leisure time available to adults and the value of moderate exercise for people of all ages, children should be encouraged to participate regularly in some form of physical activity and to cultivate interests and habits that can remain throughout life.

Since teachers of physical education frequently have responsibilities involving health education and administrative functions,[32] these areas should be included in the preparation of such teachers. Obviously, they need to be familiar with the methods and materials used in various physical education activities. Any good program to prepare physical education teachers should provide a thorough background, including such courses as anatomy, physiology, kinesiology, and chemistry. An understanding of the child and his growth and development is essential for a good physical education teacher.

The physical education teacher should have the qualities of any good teacher. However, she needs particularly to be in good health, enthusiastic, physically skilled, able in human relations, and capable of being a leader. Her work can bring much satisfac-

[29] Anna S. Espenschade, *Physical Education in the Elementary School* (Washington, D.C.: National Education Association, 1963), p. 19.
[30] *Ibid.*, p. 18.
[31] *Ibid.*, p. 19.
[32] Bucher, *op. cit.*, p. 433.

tion as she attempts ". . . to help each child develop his capacities, broaden his interests, and find joy in play."[33]

SCHOOL COUNSELING

The school counselor, along with the school psychologist and the school social worker, to be discussed later in the chapter, is a member of the pupil personnel services team.[34] Even though the counselor is concerned with the guidance function, the term *pupil personnel services* is used here because there has been a shift away from the term *school guidance*. The latter term has come to be confused and misunderstood, and the shift away from its use reflects a growing awareness that no one person can be all things to all people.[35] Today, the counselor works with a variety of specialists to provide the kinds of services that students need.

The actual work of a particular school counselor is not easy to describe because of differences among schools and among responsibilities assigned to counseling positions. Edward Roeber, acknowledging these differences, suggested that the secondary school counselor spends about 50–60 percent of his time for direct services to pupils such as counseling and working with large and small groups; 10–15 percent of his time for direct services to parents such as parent conferences and group meetings; 15–20 percent of his time for direct services to teachers and administrators such as individual consultations and case conferences; and 10–20 percent of his time for research and leadership activities such as improving testing plans and records systems and improving relations with community resource groups.[36]

The Commission on Guidance in American Schools has listed four major responsibilities for the school counselor:

[33] Espenschade, *op. cit.*, p. 27.
[34] Richard P. Koeppe and John F. Bancroft, "Elementary and Secondary School Programs," American Educational Research Association, "Guidance, Counseling, and Personnel Services," *Review of Educational Research*, 36: 219, April, 1966.
[35] *Ibid.*, p. 228.
[36] Edward C. Roeber, *Orientation to the Job of a Counselor* (Chicago: Science Research Associates, 1961), p. 13.

a. *counseling [with] students* on matters of self-understanding, decision-making, and planning, using both the interview and group situations;

b. *consulting with staff and parents* on questions of student understanding and student management;

c. *studying changes in the character of the student population* and [making a continuing interpretation of] this information [to] the school [administration] and to curriculum-development committees;

d. *performing a liaison function* between other school and community counseling resources and facilitating their use by teachers and students.[37]

In order to function effectively, the counselor has to be well prepared for his work. To be certified in almost all states, a prospective counselor has to have had teaching experience. Thus, counseling education will be undertaken at the graduate level, and in some institutions the program is a two-year one. The program should include much work in psychology and the social sciences; developing an understanding of educational philosophy and school curriculum patterns; applied or technique courses such as counseling and measurement; supervised experience; developing a basic understanding of research methods; and an introduction to the ethical and legal responsibilities in counseling.[38]

The position of secondary school counselor is fairly well established, but the position of elementary school counselor is a relatively new one. There are some differences of opinion as to just what functions the elementary school counselor should perform. One group sees him as a professional person who will provide services to all pupils and whose education can be similar to that of secondary school counselors; another group sees his major contribution as that of consulting with teachers, parents, and principals about children who have learning problems. This latter group also feels that the education of the elementary school coun-

[37] C. Gilbert Wrenn, *The Counselor in a Changing World* (Washington, D.C.: American Personnel and Guidance Association, 1962), p. 141.
[38] *Ibid.*, pp. 167–168.

selor should be different from that of the secondary school counselor.[39] Furthermore, the Commission on Guidance in American Schools indicated that the elementary school counselor has three specialized capacities: nonverbal communication with children; skills in reading diagnosis and accompanying emotional problems; skill in working with parents individually and in small groups.[40]

Many of the desirable characteristics of a school counselor are similar to those of an effective teacher. He surely must be mature, emotionally stable, and have much self-knowledge and understanding; he must really know, like, and understand young people; he must have good judgment and common sense; he must have leadership qualities and a wholesome philosophy of life; he must have a strong sense of professional ethics and a dedication to his work. All of this he must have, for he works with and influences the growth of human personalities.

SCHOOL PSYCHOLOGY

School psychology is so new as a profession that its roles are not yet uniformly defined, nor are the services it should provide fully agreed upon. Essentially, school psychologists apply the principles and techniques of psychology to educational problems within the school setting. There are, unfortunately, not enough school psychologists; too many young people do not have access to these specialists.[41]

The school psychologist needs to have preparation in both psychology and education. While most school psychologists are presently trained at the one- or two-year graduate level, the doctorate will surely become the standard of the future.[42] Persons aspiring to work in the field of school psychology should have high intelli-

---

[39] Koeppe and Bancroft, op. cit., p. 229.
[40] Wrenn, op. cit., p. 150.
[41] Paul E. Eiserer, The School Psychologist, The Library of Education (Washington, D.C.: The Center for Applied Research in Education, 1963), pp. 1–5.
[42] Ibid., p. 6.

gence, fine character, maturity, a strong desire to assist young people, and an interest in applying the science of psychology in a school setting. Unable or disinterested people in a number of educational positions can do harm to young people, but probably no position is more dangerous in this sense than the position of school psychologist. Very able and dedicated practitioners are a must in the field of school psychology.

The school psychologist works cooperatively with other school personnel such as the school counselor, the school social worker, reading and speech specialists, the school nurse, administrators, and classroom teachers. His primary roles are those of assessment and remediation. He assesses the abilities, aptitudes, interests, achievements, personality, and adjustment of individual students. Young people are usually referred to the school psychologist because of difficulties in learning, behavior problems in the classroom, or personality disorders. It is his job to diagnose the difficulties and determine remedial steps to be taken. He will make use of all possible data in an intensive study, a *case study*, of a particular youngster and his problem. He may make classroom observations of the student and conduct interviews with the child, his teacher, and perhaps the parents and the principal.

After his study, the school psychologist will probably confer with the child's classroom teacher to discuss remedial steps. The teacher may be an important factor, because remediation usually involves changes in the people and circumstances that brought about the problem as well as changes in the child himself. For younger children, the school psychologist may use play therapy; for older children, a counseling program may be used. Perhaps some sort of group therapy may be utilized.

In his consultant role, the school psychologist works not only with the educational staff but also with parents. Parents can often provide important information about a youngster and assist in a remedial program. Then too, parental problems that are complicating the student's problems can sometimes be identified. His consultant role is expanding in some schools where the school psychologist is helping to improve the functioning of teachers within the classroom. He can bring much knowledge of human growth and development to the teacher as well as knowledge of how groups can function better within the school. He can also assist teachers to function more effectively as persons through increased self-knowledge and insight into their behavior and the behavior of others.

There are other tasks that the school psychologist must undertake. He must complete a number of reports on particular students. Continually, he adds information to the records kept on students. (These records are best if they are cumulative, i.e., if the records contain information about the child's complete school career chronologically.) He frequently is called upon to classify pupils for special education.[43] In the future, the school psychologist will probably be more involved in the research function in both active and consultative roles.[44]

SCHOOL SOCIAL WORK

A relatively new member of the pupil personnel services team is the school social worker, who attempts to use the methods of social work to help children ". . . whose problems in school stem from social and emotional causes within the child, his home, or some other area of his environment."[45] The school social worker searches for the causes of the youngster's difficulties and makes an effort to remedy or at least modify the situation. In doing so, he may often work directly with the child, his teacher, and his parents.

Who are the children and young people to whom the school social worker renders service? They are the emotionally immature; those with poor social adjustments; those who dislike school, are disinterested, and are frequently absent; those who are resentful toward discipline and authority; and others who are not

[43] These pupils are discussed in Chapter 9 under "Exceptional Children."
[44] Eiserer, *passim.*
[45] Joseph P. Hourihan, "School Social Work Services," Frances C. Rosecrance and Velma D. Hayden, *School Guidance and Personnel Services* (Boston: Allyn and Bacon, 1960), pp. 138–139.

achieving as they should because of social and emotional problems. These problems may be due to the child's attitudes or personality or such factors as an alcoholic parent, a broken home, trouble with the law, or a pregnancy for a high school girl.

The four types of services provided by the school social worker are casework, collaboration, coordination, and consultation.[46] Most of the worker's time, however, is spent on casework and consultation.[47] In casework, he works directly with the child and has frequent conferences with the child's parents and teachers. While regularly scheduled casework interviews are part of the procedure, each youngster and situation may present variations that require different procedures. In his first contact with the home, the worker explains the nature of school social work services and secures the parents' permission to work on the case. Then, in addition to his interviews with the child, he makes use of all the school's records on the youngster and perhaps observes him in a classroom or playground situation. Next, a plan is developed which, it is hoped, will bring about a better school adjustment for the child. The school social worker may well involve other community agencies in the case, if such agencies have been or are presently working with the child or the family.

In consultative cases, the school social worker does not work directly with the child, but he frequently holds conferences with the classroom teacher and other school personnel about the child. Here, the classroom teacher carries the main responsibility for improving the child's adjustment with the assistance of the school social worker. In cooperative cases, the school social worker serves as liaison between the school and other community agencies which have the major responsibility for a case. The school social worker, in supportive cases, ". . . sees the child from time to time for the purpose of supporting him in his school adjustment."[48]

[46] Jerry L. Kelley, "Children with Problems: What Does the School Social Worker Do?" *NEA Journal*, 51:57, January, 1962.
[47] Hourihan, *op. cit.*, p. 145.
[48] Hourihan, *loc. cit.*

The school social worker needs to have all the qualities of other workers in the field of pupil personnel services such as the school counselor and the school psychologist, previously discussed. He, however, needs particular skill in interpersonal relations, for almost all of his time is spent in dealing with others. He needs to have the training and experience of both a teacher and a social caseworker; this usually requires two years of graduate study. The work is not without its difficulties and disappointments. The hours may be irregular and may include evening and weekend calls. The school social worker must carry, at times, quite an emotional load in continually working with young people's problems. And he has his share of failures and discouragement. However, he has the opportunity to render real service and to achieve real satisfaction.

SPEECH THERAPY

There is much need for speech therapists to work with the more than two million school children who have impaired speech. The field of speech correction is relatively new in the public schools, the first such program having been established in New York in 1908. But the program has grown greatly and so has the demand for speech clinicians. Speech handicapped children represent the largest group in the area of special education in our public elementary and secondary schools.[49]

What is the work of the speech therapist? What areas come under his responsibility? The speech therapist is responsible for the diagnosis and appraisal of a particular speech handicap; the development of a retraining program; the encouragement of cooperative activity on the part of those involved in the problem (the child, the parents, the speech therapist, the classroom teacher, doctors, nurses, and so forth); the dissemination of information to all those involved; and the interpretation of the profession to the general public.[50]

[49] Wendell Johnson and Dorothy Moeller, eds., *Speech Handicapped School Children,* Third edition (New York: Harper & Row, Publishers, 1967), p. 2.
[50] *Ibid.,* p. 451.

In addition to the program of speech therapy, a speech improvement program can be instituted for children with minor speech and voice deviations. Such a program can help to decrease the number of children needing speech therapy. The classroom teacher can carry out the speech improvement program with the assistance of the therapist. The therapist thus serves as a consultant and provider of in-service training for teachers, a designer of the speech improvement curriculum, and a coordinator of speech improvement with the regular curriculum and the remedial speech program.[51]

Being a good speech therapist requires much. One has to have a thorough academic preparation at the undergraduate level, and graduate training is desirable; the ability to work with people in individual and group settings; much understanding and an infinite amount of patience; maturity and the ability to work with little supervision; a pleasing personality; and a real desire to help children.

There are difficulties in the work. For one thing, the caseload of children is frequently high. There are many records to keep and reports to make out, both of which are very important. Relations with parents are not always easy or smooth. Some parents may not readily accept the fact of their child's problem, nor may they be fully cooperative. Teachers are not always "happy" to have children leave the classroom for therapy sessions. And administrators and the general public do not always understand the nature of nor the value of a good speech therapy program. However, the work of the speech therapist in the public schools is both important and necessary. Able and dedicated people are needed.

The discussion of careers in this chapter has taken into account only some ten areas. There are many more areas and numerous

---

[51] Theodore D. Hanley and Frederic L. Darley, "Summary: New Horizons," Research Committee of the American Speech and Hearing Association, "Public School Speech and Hearing Services," *The Journal of Speech and Hearing Disorders,* Monograph Supplement 8, U.S. Office of Education Cooperative Research Project No. 649(8191), July, 1961, p. 129.

other positions in education. It is a vast field with great opportunities awaiting those with talent who wish to enter.

SUGGESTED ACTIVITIES

1. Prepare a report on the opportunities available in the area of education you have selected for your career.
2. Arrange with your instructor to have a school counselor speak to the class about his work with students.
3. Interview one of the educational workers described in this chapter to determine the aspects of his work that he finds most satisfying and those he finds least satisfying.
4. Plan with your instructor to visit a school to view the work of the administrators and those concerned with pupil personnel services. Agree as a class on the questions to be asked during your visit.
5. Read several articles on current trends in one of the teaching specialties described in this chapter. (*The Education Index* will be helpful in locating articles.) Prepare a report of your reading.
6. Dramatize in class a job interview for one of the following positions: principal, physical education teacher, or music teacher.
7. Consult materials in the library and prepare a report for class presentation on the career possibilities for some area of education not discussed in the chapter. For example, school librarian, teacher of special education, curriculum coordinator, or research worker may be a position of interest to you.
8. Form a committee to investigate the types of educational positions in your state for which there is a shortage of qualified personnel. Have the committee report to the class.

SELECTED REFERENCES

Department of Elementary School Principals. *Elementary School Principalship: A Research Study.* Thirty-seventh Yearbook. Washington, D.C.: National Education Association, 1958. A thorough consideration of the roles and responsibilities of the elementary principal, his professional opportunities and conditions of employment.

Eiserer, Paul E. *The School Psychologist.* The Library of Education. Washington, D.C.: The Center for Applied Research in Education, 1963. A good overview of the roles and functions of the school psychologist.

Fait, Hollis F. *Physical Education for the Elementary School Child.* Philadelphia: W. B. Saunders Company, 1964. A general text. See Chapter One, "Foundations of Physical Education," for a discussion of objectives and principles of physical education.

Gaitskell, Charles D. *Children and Their Art.* New York: Harcourt, Brace and Co., 1958. A comprehensive description of the teaching of art in the elementary school including methods, materials, and objectives of art education.

Goddard, Hareth B. "The Assistant Principal—Understudy or Partner in Professional Leadership," *National Association of Secondary School Principals Bulletin,* 46, No. 275:31–34 September, 1962. Analyzes the assistant principal's responsibilities.

Goldman, Samuel. *The School Principal.* The Library of Education. New York: The Center for Applied Research in Education, Inc., 1966. Discusses the responsibilities and functions of the school principal.

Green, John A. *Fields of Teaching and Educational Services.* New York: Harper & Row, Publishers, 1966. A good source of information about a number of career fields in education.

Griffiths, Daniel E. *The School Superintendent.* The Library of Education. New York: The Center for Applied Research in Education, 1966. The qualifications, responsibilities, and career opportunities of the school superintendency.

Herndon, Frank M. "A Career in Teaching the Business Subjects," *Business Education Forum,* 18:7–9, January, 1964. Presents information on the nature of the work, the opportunities available, and on the preparation and qualifications required.

Hourihan, Joseph P. "School Social Work Services," pp. 138–165. Rosecrance, Francis C., and Hayden, Velma D. *School Guidance and Personnel Services.* Boston: Allyn and Bacon, 1960. Discusses the role and functions of the school social worker.

Institute for Research. *Trade and Vocational Teaching As a Career.* Careers Research Monograph No. 231. Chicago: the Institute, 1966. Trade and industrial education is considered as a career. The requirements, opportunities, and attractive and unattractive features of such a career are discussed.

Johnson, Wendell, and Moeller, Dorothy., eds. *Speech Handicapped School Children.* Third edition. New York: Harper & Row, Publishers, 1967. A comprehensive text. See particularly Chapter Two, "The

Clinical Point of View in Education," and Chapter Nine, "The Public School Remedial Speech Program."

Kelley, Jerry L. "Children with Problems: What Does the School Social Worker Do?" *NEA Journal*, 51:55–57, January, 1962. Describes the functions of the school social worker.

National Education Association, American Association for Health, Physical Education, and Recreation. *Careers in Physical Education for Girls: A Key to Your Future.* Washington, D.C.: National Education Association, 1964. (pamphlet) Discusses the opportunities for women in physical education.

National Education Association, American Industrial Arts Association. *A Career in Teaching Industrial Arts.* Washington, D.C.: National Education Association, n.d. (pamphlet) Briefly defines industrial arts and discusses a career in teaching the subject.

National Education Association, Music Educators National Conference. *A Career in Music Education.* Washington, D.C.: the Association, 1965. (pamphlet) Discusses several important aspects of a career in music education.

National Education Association, Research Division. *Teacher Supply and Demand in the Public Schools: 1967.* Washington, D.C., 1967. A report of the annual study of teacher supply and demand in various subjects, grade levels, and geographic areas.

National Education Association. *Teaching Career Fact Book.* Washington, D.C.: the Association, 1966. A helpful guide in considering teaching as a career. Contains information on teacher supply and demand, preparation and certification, salaries, conditions of work, and other related areas. Good list of sources for further information.

Nolan, C. A., Hayden, Carlos K., and Malsbary, Dean R. *Principles and Problems of Business Education.* Third edition. Cincinnati, Ohio: South-Western Publishing Company, 1967. A comprehensive text. See particularly Part I, "Business Education, an Overview," for a discussion of the nature and purpose of business education, its developments, and its present status.

Nye, Robert Evans, and Nye, Vernice Trousdale. *Music in the Elementary School.* Second edition. Englewood Cliffs, N.J.: Prentice Hall, 1964. A methods and materials book for elementary school music. See particularly Chapter I, "An Introduction to Music Education."

Purkey, Ernest, and others. "Special Feature on Guidance," *NEA*

Journal, 51:18–30, December, 1962. Series of articles which deals with the functions of guidance personnel in elementary and secondary schools.

Research Committee of the American Speech and Hearing Association. "Public School Speech and Hearing Services," *The Journal of Speech and Hearing Disorders,* Monograph Supplement 8, U.S. Office of Education Cooperative Research Project No. 649 (8191), July, 1961. A report of the findings of a national survey on public school speech and hearing services. Presents practices, unresolved problems, and needed research.

Roeber, Edward C. *The School Counselor.* The Library of Education. Washington, D.C.: The Center for Applied Research in Education, 1963. Functions and responsibilities of the school counselor.

Singleton, Ira C. *Music in Secondary Schools.* Boston: Allyn and Bacon, 1963. A methods book for teaching music in the junior and senior high schools. Part One, "Music Education Today," may be of particular interest.

U.S. Office of Education. *Employment Outlook for Teachers.* Washington, D.C.: Government Printing Office, 1967. Annual summary of employment outlook for teachers at all levels of education.

Wrenn, C. Gilbert. *The Counselor in a Changing World.* Washington, D.C.: American Personnel and Guidance Association, 1962. A view of the future of society, of education, and of the role and preparation of the professional counselor.

Wynn, D. Richard. *Careers in Education.* New York: McGraw-Hill Book Company, 1960. Discusses employment opportunities, salaries, and other conditions of work in various educational careers.

9 Teaching All Children and Youth

Schools today are concerned with teaching all children and youth, for American education is committed to developing each student to the maximum of his learning potential, whatever that potential may be. But students differ in many ways—in intelligence, perception, motivation, personality, physical characteristics, rate of learning, and social and economic background. Furthermore, since the school now serves "all the children of all the people," the range of individual differences represented by the school's clientele is greater than ever before. Is it any wonder, then, that teaching today's young people is a difficult and complex task?

Much of what has been said in this book so far about teaching has been said with reference to the average student. One quickly learns in teaching, however, that there is no such thing as the "average" student. Each child differs from all others in some ways. Ideally, each child should be taught individually, but the practicalities of time, staff, facilities, and money make this virtually impossible. Many students, though, differ from the norm to such an extent that they do require special attention. It seems appropriate, therefore, to focus on these students in this last chapter. Attention will be directed to two groups of such students: exceptional children and youth and the socially and culturally disadvantaged.

184

EXCEPTIONAL CHILDREN AND YOUTH

Who is the exceptional child? This is not an easy question to answer, for the term includes many different groups of young people. Cruickshank says, however, that the exceptional child is essentially

> . . . one who deviates intellectually, physically, socially, or emotionally so markedly from what is considered to be normal growth and development that he cannot receive maximum benefit from a regular school program and requires a special class or supplementary instruction and services.[1]

In other words, an exceptional child is one who deviates sufficiently from the norm so as to require special educational services. This field of education is thus known as *special education* and includes four general groups of students: the physically handicapped, the emotionally disturbed, the multi-handicapped, and the intellectually exceptional.[2]

Before going on to discuss exceptional children and what the school can do for them, it would be wise to consider briefly the practice of putting labels on youngsters. The author uses labels here to describe various groups of students for classification purposes only. It is all too easy to put a label on someone; it is not so easy for that person to overcome the consequences of labeling. A label can become derisive if it is used in the wrong way. Children are quick to pick up from their teacher, for example, a slurring remark involving a label. If she speaks of "those special children," whatever the group involved, with a certain intonation, the other students may well imitate her attitude. Too often a child will have to carry his "label" throughout most of his school career. Furthermore, a label can sometimes be used by teachers as a convenient excuse for giving up on a youngster. They say, "What's

[1] William M. Cruickshank, "The Development of Education for Exceptional Children," William M. Cruickshank and G. Orville Johnson, eds., *Education of Exceptional Children and Youth*, Second edition (Englewood Cliffs, N.J.: Prentice-Hall, 1967), pp. 3–4.

[2] Classifications used by Cruickshank, *ibid.*, pp. 3–7.

the use? Johnnie is a —— (fill in the label)." So, be most careful about labels. Do not be quick to place them on a student. Do not let the label blur your view of a child. Take him for the child he is and forget about the label!

The Physically Handicapped

The child with impaired vision is included within this group. He may be classified as partially sighted or blind, though not all classified as blind are completely without sight. For the child with impaired vision, there are special materials such as books with large print or braille and special teachers that may be provided. Attempts are made to use other senses and to provide concrete experiences in learning. Though relatively few children are affected by visual impairments, this handicap can have quite an influence on total growth and development of the child. Therefore, it is valuable for him to be in as many normal school situations as possible. The author has observed blind children, for instance, within the regular classroom who receive special tutoring and assistance from a traveling teacher of the visually impaired. In this way they are with normal children most of the time, yet they are given the special help they need.

Students with impaired hearing may be hard of hearing or deaf. Each child must be considered individually in planning a suitable educational program, though deaf children will require more specialized aid. The hard-of-hearing youngster may be placed in a regular class with an understanding teacher who is oriented to his special needs. Obviously, he will have to be seated near the teacher, and she will have to rephrase things for him. His classmates will have to be brought to understand his problem, the hearing aid he wears, and the need to use a little extra effort to be sure he hears what they are saying.

Impaired speech[3] often goes along with impaired hearing. There are a variety of speech disabilities, and children in this category represent the largest group (more than two million) in the

[3] In this connection, see the discussion of the work of the speech therapist in Chapter 8.

area of special education in our public elementary and secondary schools.[4] Among the speech problems found are ". . . problems of speech development, problems of articulation, voice, stuttering, and certain physical and environmental conditions that may be considered as special problems."[5] The classroom teacher must understand and allow for the needs of the speech-handicapped child, but she must not put too much pressure on the child for him to want to change his speech or speech patterns.[6] This is particularly true of those students with problems resulting from such factors as cleft palate or cerebral palsy. The speech therapist has primary responsibility for working with the speech handicapped, and it is the therapist who can offer valuable suggestions to the classroom teacher to enable her to give the proper supplementary assistance.

Crippled children vary not only in the nature of their handicap but also in the severity of their handicap. Some children may only be mildly disabled while others are completely incapacitated. One would find among "crippled children" those with cerebral palsy, poliomyelitis, club foot, and many other conditions and diseases. Here again the educational plan must be based upon the individual youngster and his problems. Many crippled children can be involved in the regular school program when the program is based upon individual differences and needs. "Consensus of opinion favors emphasis on normalcy in school placement, programming, and participation,"[7] when such involvement is feasible and advantageous to the disabled child and not detrimental to the nonhandicapped child.

A variety of terms is used to describe brain-injured children, who constitute a branch of special education which is just beginning to develop. Whether they are called brain-damaged chil-

[4] Wendell Johnson and Dorothy Moeller, eds., *Speech Handicapped School Children*, Third edition (New York: Harper & Row, Publishers, 1967), p. 2.
[5] Stanley H. Ainsworth, "The Education of Children with Speech Handicaps," Cruickshank and Johnson, *op. cit.*, p. 428.
[6] *Ibid.*, p. 429.
[7] Frances P. Connor, "The Education of Crippled Children," Cruickshank and Johnson, *op. cit.*, p. 499.

dren, children with cerebral dysfunction, hyperactive children, or
children with special learning difficulties, they are characterized
by visual-motor, audio-motor, and/or tactual-motor disturbances.[8]
They appear to be

> . . . clumsy, have difficulty in cutting with scissors, cutting while
> using a knife and fork, lacing shoes, writing with a pencil, or per-
> forming other learned skills which involve finger dexterity and
> coordination.[9]

The education of these youngsters is a complicated task and must
be based upon a team approach involving the clinical psychologist and a number of other specialists. While the specifics of such
an educational program are beyond the scope of this discussion,
it can be said that these children need a set routine, a consistent
relationship with their teacher, and a learning environment in
which they can experience success.[10]

The Emotionally Disturbed

Providing for socially and emotionally disturbed children and
youth is a rapidly expanding segment of special education.[11] The
problem of social and emotional maladjustment cuts across all
groups of young people. Though the exact number affected by
the problem is not known, it is estimated at two and a half million to four and a half million.[12] Unfortunately, the vast majority
of these children and youth are in the regular classroom where
they receive little or no special help. Too often many of these students are seen by teachers simply as troublemakers and not as the
mentally unwell people they are. However, it is not always easy
to identify disturbed children; normal children show symptoms of
the disturbed at times, and disturbed youngsters function nor-

---

[8] William M. Cruickshank, "The Education of the Child with Brain Injury,"
Cruickshank and Johnson, *op. cit.*, p. 239.
[9] *Loc. cit.*
[10] *Ibid.*, p. 275.
[11] William C. Morse, "The Education of Socially Maladjusted and Emotionally Disturbed Children," Cruickshank and Johnson, *op. cit.*, p. 569.
[12] *Ibid.*, p. 571.

mally in certain areas of behavior. Those included in the category of social and emotional maladjustment range from children who have not developed fully socially and cannot relate well or show feeling for others, through the neurotic, to those who are seriously disturbed, the psychotic. The deeply disturbed should not be within the province of the classroom teacher; those not so deeply disturbed may receive psychological therapy and be able to function in a special school setting; and those least disturbed may function adequately in the regular classroom.

The teacher of maladjusted children and youth must respond to the "why" of the young person's behavior more than to the behavior itself. The major goal is to help the student to feel more hopeful and to reduce anxiety to a nonpainful level.[13] "Teaching disturbed children," however, "should be recognized for what it is, a wearing experience to the most mature and adequate teacher."[14] A key question, of course, is when the disturbed child should be removed from the regular classroom. The answer depends upon what removal would mean in terms of the child, the group, and the teacher. If the child's needs cannot be met in the regular class, he should be removed. He should also be removed if his behavior presents too much of a problem for the rest of the class. The ability of the particular teacher to handle the youngster is a factor, and so are the feelings and perceptions of the child and his family.[15] While the school is surely concerned with mental health, it is not primarily an institution for therapy. Therapeutic work must be consigned to those qualified to undertake this difficult task.

The Multi-handicapped

It is not unusual to find an exceptional child with multiple handicaps. "The largest group of multiple handicapped children is characterized by mental retardation in relation to another phys-

[13] *Ibid.*, p. 595.
[14] *Ibid.*, p. 597.
[15] *Ibid.*, p. 609.

ical disability."[16] Others may have a combination of emotional and physical disabilities; still others may have two or more physical disabilities such as impaired vision and speech. Currently, much thought is being given to the education of the multi-handicapped, though insufficient research has been done in this area of special education.

Before going on to discuss the last general group of exceptional children, the intellectually exceptional, perhaps two general comments should be made. The first is that in recent literature on special education, increased emphasis is being placed on the need to group for instruction on the basis of common educational problems or needs, rather than on the basis of a rigid classification of exceptionality.[17] In other words, the educational needs of children are generally a better basis for grouping than are their disabilities. Secondly, there seems to be a trend to place the exceptional child in the regular classroom as much as possible.

The Intellectually Exceptional

Classed as intellectually exceptional are children at the extremes of the intelligence scale: the gifted at the high end and the slow learners and the mentally retarded at the other end. Attention will be directed first to the mentally retarded and the slow learner; then a more extended section will be given over to the gifted because of the increased interest evidenced in recent years about such students.

For educational purposes the mentally retarded may be divided into the trainable and the educable. The trainable mentally retarded have IQ's ranging from 25 or 30 to 50 or 55; the educable mentally retarded range in IQ from 55 or 60 to 80. The slow learner IQ range is 80 to 95. Each of these ranges, however, is approximate. The measured characteristics of a particular child

---

[16] William M. Cruickshank, "The Development of Education for Exceptional Children," Cruickshank and Johnson, *op. cit.*, p. 7.

[17] See, for example, American Educational Research Association, "Education of Exceptional Children," *Review of Educational Research,* Vol. 36, No. 1, February, 1966.

are more important in determining where he falls in the spectrum of retardation.

The trainable mentally retarded are not capable of being educated in the sense that they can learn academic skills to any degree of proficiency. It is only recently that they have been considered a responsibility of the public school.[18] These children will require care and supervision for their entire lives. The school can help them to learn some habits of health, safety, and self-care. Perhaps limited use of transportation facilities and recognition of appropriate signs found in daily living can also be taught. The hope is to make the trainable mentally retarded as effective and competent as is possible within their severe limitations.

In contrast to the 0.3 percent of the population that the trainable mentally retarded constitute, the educable mentally retarded make up 2 to 3 percent of the total school population.[19] The special classes in the elementary and secondary schools for these children exist basically because of their deviation from normal in intellectual growth, for most educable retarded children are within the normal range in most of the other areas of their development.[20] With a proper program these young people can achieve social and economic independence as adults. They can acquire academic skills and sufficient training to secure and hold an income-producing position.

The teacher of the mentally retarded should be thoroughly trained to work with such students. She should have a sound background in the education of normal children in addition to her special skills. She can help these children to be happier human beings, to do things for themselves, to be easier to live with, to have better speech, and to be better coordinated.

The slow learners, who constitute from 15 to 17 percent of the school population,[21] usually have been accommodated in the regular classroom. Much attention has been given to this group in

[18] G. Orville Johnson, "The Education of Mentally Retarded Children," Cruickshank and Johnson, *op. cit.*, p. 195.

[19] *Ibid.*, p. 234.

[20] *Ibid.*, p. 201.

[21] *Ibid.*, p. 195.

recent years because of their high dropout rate, truancy, high incidence of delinquency, and receipt of public relief.[22] These students "... provide one of the largest and most intense, continuing problems facing the classroom teacher."[23] They cannot "keep up" with the rest of the class, and they fall farther and farther behind. Often the problem is misunderstood by teachers and some administrators. What has clouded the issue is that many children have been called "slow learners" when, in fact, their problems were due to other causes. They may have been slow in learning, but they were not slow learners. Slow learners are retarded in their intellectual development. Though the retardation is not severe, it is sufficient to cause them to have difficulty in a school program planned for children of normal intelligence. There is a limit to their mental growth. Johnson places their maximum mental growth in a range from 11 years to 13 years, 6 months.[24] However, they can learn, though they will grasp skills and concepts more slowly than students in general. They usually are poor readers and have a short attention span, but they do not look physically different from the average student. Their school life has generally been one of continuous frustration and failure, filled with meaningless activities. Is it any wonder that they do not like school!

Elementary schools have done a better job with the slow learners than have the secondary schools, for good elementary schools individualize instruction. Use is made of student interest and experience in learning. Small groups are formed within the class. Emphasis is placed upon fundamental skills, yet personal relationships are also stressed. All of these things have value for the slow learner. In the secondary schools, where the problem is newer, less has been done in general. When slow learners are grouped together in a separate class, often the same textbook is

[22] G. Orville Johnson, *Education for the Slow Learners* (Englewood Cliffs, N.J.: Prentice-Hall, 1963).
[23] *Ibid.*, p. 9.
[24] *Ibid.*, p. 10.

used that is used in the regular class. Though the content is "watered down," it still consists of the same basic materials and experiences provided for the average class. This is done in spite of the fact that the slow learner may not be able to read or benefit from the textbook and that the materials and experiences may not be appropriate for him.[25] Surely much needs to be done to improve the situation for slow learners, particularly in the secondary school.

The Gifted

Who the gifted are depends upon the definition one uses. "The common element in most of the large number of definitions of a gifted child," however, "is 'intellectual ability' as measured by some form of intelligence test."[26] For example, Lewis Terman, a pioneer in the study of the gifted,[27] defines the gifted as those with an IQ of 140 or higher on the Stanford-Binet Intelligence Scale. Using the same scale, Leta Hollingworth included in her gifted group only children with an IQ of 180 or above.[28] (This definition would include about one child in a million!) In a broader definition, Robert DeHaan and Robert Havighurst describe the gifted child as one who ". . . is superior in some ability that can make him an outstanding contributor to the welfare of, and quality of living in society."[29] Others would include students of outstanding skill and talent in many areas such as music, art, dance, creative writing, and leadership. Consequently, the term *gifted child* may mean a number of things.

There are difficulties in using IQ to determine who is gifted. An IQ score, for instance, does not have real meaning unless one

[25] *Ibid.*, p. 25.
[26] James J. Gallagher, *The Gifted Child in the Elementary School* (Washington, D.C.: National Education Association, 1959), p. 3.
[27] Lewis M. Terman and others, *Genetic Studies of Genius,* Vols. I–IV (Stanford, Calif.: Stanford University Press, 1925–47).
[28] Leta S. Hollingworth, *Children Above 180 I.Q.* (Tarrytown, N.Y.: World Book Co., 1942)
[29] Robert F. DeHaan and Robert J. Havighurst, *Educating Gifted Children,* Revised edition (Chicago: University of Chicago Press, 1961), p. 15.

knows the particular test that was administered. This is especially true at the extreme levels, so that an IQ of 130, for instance, is not always "130."[30] Furthermore:

> The fact that intelligence is now generally accepted as multidimensional means that one cannot expect to give one respected intelligence test and have that used as an operational definition of giftedness. The fact that IQ scores are now considered to vary with development and experience means that one measure of ability, at a given point in time, is not sufficient for a definition. Finally, the fact that IQ scores are considered partially the result of learned experiences means that the past and possible future experiences of the individual have to be taken into account for a total evaluation. This last part has direct relevance to the person whom we call the culturally deprived or disadvantaged child.[31]

A gifted child who is culturally deprived, therefore, may not be identified through the use of an IQ test. Students with reading difficulties, emotional problems, or low motivation may also not reveal their true capacity on intelligence tests.

In addition to group and individual intelligence tests, teacher observation, achievement tests, and tests of "creativity" are also used to identify the gifted. Each of these devices alone has limitations as a measuring instrument. Classroom teachers, for example, identify as gifted many students who are not gifted according to individualized tests. More importantly, teachers do not identify some children whom tests indicate are intellectually gifted.[32] Tests of "creativity" are new and not yet sufficiently reliable as identification instruments. These tests attempt to identify those who think along divergent lines, i.e., those whose thinking includes characteristics of fluency, flexibility, and foresight. Gallagher believes that such tests ". . . will almost surely change the operational definition of gifted children."[33]

[30] Gallagher, *op. cit.*, pp. 6–7.
[31] James J. Gallagher, *Teaching the Gifted Child* (Boston: Allyn and Bacon, 1964), p. 6.
[32] Gallagher, *The Gifted Child in the Elementary School*, p. 8.
[33] Gallagher, *Teaching the Gifted Child*, p. 42.

The skills and talents gifted youngsters possess can be stated as follows:

1. The ability to associate and interrelate concepts.
2. The ability to evaluate facts and arguments critically.
3. The ability to create new ideas and originate new lines of thought.
4. The ability to reason through complex problems.
5. The ability to understand other situations, other times, and other people, to be less bound by one's own peculiar environmental surroundings.[34]

For some time, it was thought that gifted students were different from others.

The myth of the gifted child as a queer, physically weak little prodigy who became neurotic and was apt to burn out quickly persisted for many years. This stereotype can no longer be accepted. Instead of being puny, nearsighted little misfits, these children are sturdy, vivacious, fun-loving, well-adjusted youngsters.[35]

While these generalizations are true,

. . . the teacher will know that children do not arrive in his classroom in averages. The important fact for the teacher to reflect on is that gifted and creative children can come in every shape, size, color, and family background.[36]

The gifted have generally been provided for by means of enrichment, acceleration, special classes or teachers, or other special grouping arrangements. *Enrichment* is an attempt to provide for the gifted within the regular classroom and is probably the most common method used with gifted students.[37] Theoretically, the able youngster is given "enriched" learning experiences in which

[34] *Ibid.*, p. 80.
[35] Gertrude H. Hildreth, *Introduction to the Gifted* (New York: McGraw-Hill Book Company, 1966), p. 68.
[36] Gallagher, *Teaching the Gifted Child,* pp. 9–10.
[37] Robert F. DeHaan, *Accelerated Learning Programs,* The Library of Education (Washington, D.C.: The Center for Applied Research in Education, 1963), p. 46.

he deals with advanced subject matter or probes material more deeply. Too often, however, the gifted student has simply been given more of the same work. If he finishes the five assigned arithmetic problems before the rest of the class, for instance, the teacher will tell him to do the next five problems, rather than to prepare special work for him or permit him to work on his own.

Acceleration is a plan by which the gifted may complete school more quickly or at a younger age. It may take such forms as early admission to first grade, ungraded primary, skipping grades, heavier programs per year for high school students, or advanced placement programs. Grade skipping is probably the least desirable method of acceleration, for it can present problems of social and emotional adjustment. However, James Gallagher states that

> the available research indicates clearly that moderate acceleration in the elementary school does no noticeable harm to the gifted child, and has shortened his academic operation by one-half to one year.[38]

Through acceleration at the high school level, a gifted student can shorten his time in secondary school by perhaps one year. He can do this by carrying a heavier program each year and by attending summer school. Many high schools also participate in the Advanced Placement Program conducted under the auspices of the College Entrance Examination Board. Under this program, college-level courses are offered by secondary schools in a number of subjects to gifted high school students. Upon completion of the courses and the advanced placement examinations, students may be given college credit for the courses or advanced standing upon admission. If a student has completed a sufficient number of such courses, he may be admitted to college as a sophomore, thus shortening his college stay to three years.

Grouping gifted students separately for instruction is often advocated as a means of meeting their needs. The question of grouping has been a perennial one in education and has implications for all students. Students may be grouped for instruction heterogeneously or homogeneously. Heterogeneous grouping is

[38] Gallagher, *The Gifted Child in the Elementary School*, p. 25.

simply grouping students by age for each grade level and perhaps by alphabetical order for each class or section. Homogeneous grouping, on the other hand, involves grouping students by some set of criteria supposedly related to their ability to learn. Usually such things as IQ, reading skill, scholastic averages, achievement test scores, and teacher recommendations are used as criteria. (Actually, there is no truly homogeneous group, for no two people are exactly alike.)

One can find equally persuasive arguments and research for and against grouping by ability. For instance, such grouping is held to be democratic or undemocratic, fair or unfair, better for students or worse for students, better for teachers or worse for teachers. Regardless of the arguments, ability grouping in some form appears to be widely used today, as Dr. Conant discovered in his study of the comprehensive high school.[39] Perhaps it would be good, however, to distinguish grouping rigidly across the board from grouping flexibly, say by subject or special need. Rigid grouping leads to the problem of labeling youngsters again. Whether you call the groups "slow," "average," and "fast" in high school or "robins," "blue jays," and "chickadees" for primary grade reading groups, it does not take long for those in the low group, the "chickadees," to realize that they are the "dumb" group. And, as was said before, labels are hard to lose.

In a more flexible type of grouping, say by subject in the secondary school, the problem of labeling is lessened. A student may be in the top group in English, the second group in mathematics, the third group in social studies, the second group in biology, the top group in foreign language, and ungrouped for art or music and physical education. The Dual Progress Plan,[40] discussed in Chapter 7, is an attempt at flexible grouping in the elementary school. In this plan, youngsters are grouped by grade level for half of the school day in language arts and social studies and

[39] James B. Conant, *The Comprehensive High School: A Second Report to Interested Citizens* (New York: McGraw-Hill Book Company, 1967), p. 67.

[40] George D. Stoddard, *The Dual Progress Plan* (New York: Harper & Brothers, 1961).

198   FOCUS ON TEACHING

grouped by ability in other subjects for the balance of the day. Of
course, there are problems with any grouping plan, but each plan
represents an attempt to decrease the range of individual differences for instructional purposes.

In summing up our discussion of the ways of providing for
gifted students, it would be fair to say that each of the three
plans used—enrichment, acceleration, and grouping—is workable
and acceptable under certain conditions.[41] How well any plan
works depends upon the competence of the faculty and the determination of both faculty and administration to make the plan
work. The approach of the faculty must be experimental, and
concern for the individual student and his needs must be
paramount.[42]

Authorities differ as to which plan should be used for educating the gifted, however. James Dunlop recommends the use of all
three plans in teaching the gifted student.[43] James Gallagher believes that enrichment ". . . is slowly being abandoned in favor
of more extensive provisions."[44] And he further believes that acceleration and grouping have more value if special curriculum
modifications are also made.[45] It makes little sense to group students by ability and still make use of the same curriculum for all
groups. In the end, the question seems to be not so much which
plan to use as it is how well the plan is implemented, how well it
meets the needs of the students involved.

THE SOCIALLY AND CULTURALLY DISADVANTAGED

A whole literature has developed about the disadvantaged
American, the American who is socially and culturally deprived

[41] DeHaan, *op. cit.*, p. 47.
[42] *Loc. cit.*
[43] James M. Dunlop, "The Education of Children with High Mental Ability," William M. Cruickshank and G. Orville Johnson, eds., *Education of
Exceptional Children and Youth,* Second edition (Englewood Cliffs, N.J.:
Prentice-Hall, 1967), p. 186.
[44] Gallagher, *Teaching the Gifted Child*, p. 95.
[45] *Ibid.*, p. 96.

of what the average middle-class person takes for granted. There are millions of poor children in the nation's schools who are the children of the disadvantaged. Their problems and the things that the school can and should be doing about these problems are many and complex. This discussion will be limited to an attempt to answer briefly two questions: Who are the disadvantaged? What can be done to meet their needs?

Who Are the Disadvantaged?

"There is probably no typical 'socially disadvantaged child' but instead a wide variety of such children with widely varying characteristics."[46] For purposes of discussion, though, it is necessary to make certain generalizations about the disadvantaged. Michael Harrington, who writes movingly of the disadvantaged in his book *The Other America: Poverty in the United States,* describes the main subcultures of poverty as the aged, the minorities, the agricultural workers, and the industrial rejects.[47] Thus, poverty is found not only in urban areas but in rural areas as well. And the people who live in poverty are different—they live differently and feel different:

> The other Americans feel differently than the rest of the nation. They tend to be hopeless and passive, yet prone to bursts of violence; they are lonely and isolated, often rigid and hostile. To be poor is not simply to be deprived of the material things of this world. It is to enter a fatal, futile universe, an America within America with a twisted spirit.[48]

Poverty is not solely a Negro problem, for Negroes probably make up only about 25 percent of the disadvantaged. But Negroes, as members of a racial minority, are particularly disadvantaged:

[46] Edmund W. Gordon, "Characteristics of Socially Disadvantaged Children," American Educational Research Association, "Education for Socially Disadvantaged Children," *Review of Educational Research,* Vol. 35, No. 6: 385, December, 1965.

[47] Michael Harrington, *The Other America: Poverty in the United States* (Baltimore: Penguin Books, 1963), p. 180.

[48] *Ibid.,* p. 120.

To belong to a racial minority is to be poor, but poor in a special way. The fear, the lack of self-confidence, the haunting, these have been described. But they, in turn, are the expression of the most institutionalized poverty in the United States, the most vicious of the vicious circles. In a sense, the Negro is classically the "other" American, degraded and frustrated at every turn and not just because of laws.[49]

The problems of the Negro have been much in the news in recent years. Money, time, and effort have been expended in an attempt to solve these problems. However, the Negro still finds himself discriminated against, still finds his children in poor schools, and still finds himself in the ghetto.

The culture of the disadvantaged differs in many ways from that of middle-class America. In presenting a "portrait" of the underprivileged, Frank Riessman details some of the following characteristics: the disadvantaged person is traditional, superstitious, somewhat religious, and a poor reader; his opinions about morality, punishment, the role of women, and intellectuals are inflexible and not open to reason; he is not individualistic, self-oriented, or concerned with self-expression; he sees the world as responsible for his troubles rather than himself; he wants to "get by" rather than "get ahead"; he is prejudiced, intolerant, and likes strong leaders; he values highly his family and personal comforts; he is pragmatic and anti-intellectual; he admires strength and endurance and those things he considers masculine.[50] The family may be broken by divorce or desertion, but some homes tend to be overcrowded because they include many relatives (the extended family). The inadequacy of the housing facilities is much publicized; the role of the family as a source of security and protection, however, is less well known. Frequently, though, both parents may work, resulting in the neglect of the children. Physical punishment is often used to maintain discipline.

Many of the things that the disadvantaged child learns in the family ill equip him for school:

[49] *Ibid.*, p. 73.
[50] Frank Riessman, *The Culturally Deprived Child* (New York: Harper & Row, Publishers, 1962), pp. 26–30.

Pupils from extended families in the slum are often unfamiliar with scheduling, time limits, and assignment deadlines. In the absence of planning at home and with little background in making decisions, they find themselves in difficulty when confronted with deliberative situations in which circumstance does not choose for them but rather they themselves must decide alone.[51]

Furthermore, because conformity is valued in the home, ". . . the incentive system of working against others is unlikely to motivate such children and neither will failure bring a zealous search for knowledge."[52] The school, in general, is not supported by the home. As a result,

. . . there is little preparation in the home for the child's school experience, little contribution to the child's understanding of what it is or what it can do for him, and little day-to-day reinforcement through the home of the progress which the school attempts to achieve.[53]

The disadvantaged child brings to school an impoverished vocabulary along with a negative attitude and aggressive behavior. Actually, ". . . he may enter the first grade without ever having seen a person read and with no knowledge of what the reading experience means."[54] He starts school with deficiencies and tends to fall farther behind as he goes through the grades. In addition to his vocabulary problem, which makes it difficult for him to handle abstractions, the experience of the disadvantaged child has given him stunted social attitudes and low intellectual and vocational aspirations.[55]

What Can Be Done to Meet the Needs of the Disadvantaged?

A detailed description of the things that can be done for the

[51] Robert D. Strom, *Teaching in the Slum School* (Columbus, Ohio: Charles E. Merrill Books, 1965), p. 36.
[52] *Loc. cit.*
[53] Educational Policies Commission, *American Education and the Search for Equal Opportunity* (Washington, D.C.: National Education Association, 1965), p. 5.
[54] *Loc. cit.*
[55] *Ibid.*, p. 7.

disadvantaged is beyond the scope of this discussion. Some illustrative suggestions for programs and practices will be reviewed.
Ample references are available at the end of the chapter for further investigation.

The Educational Policies Commission has recommended that
". . . nursery and kindergarten education for disadvantaged children should be available everywhere at public expense."[56] Such
education should provide the necessary experience and stimula-
tion to develop readiness for learning. The Commission further
suggests that the grade-level barrier be removed in order to individualize instruction more and decrease rigidity in school systems.
The importance of knowing each child is stressed as well as the
need to give each student a sense of his own worth. Emphasis is
also placed upon developing the essential skill of reading for the
disadvantaged child. To do these kinds of things teachers need
freedom to plan and experiment on their own.[57] The Commission
also draws attention to the need to provide adult and continuing
education for the disadvantaged. This kind of program needs to be
different from the regular school program, for

> . . . it is necessary that the schooling be appropriate to the student's
> age. A thirty-year-old fifth grader cannot be treated in the same way
> as a ten-year-old, and there may be little use in bringing a dropout
> back to the same program from which he once fled by quitting
> school.[58]

Professor Riessman, in his book *The Culturally Deprived
Child*, makes a number of suggestions for the education of the
disadvantaged. Some of the more important points that he makes
are: the need to understand and respect the disadvantaged child
and the culture from which he comes; the need to focus more on
the positive aspects of the culture of poverty (the value of the
family and informal, comfortable relationships with people, for
example); and the fact that the disadvantaged are not so much
against education as they are against the school which

---

[56] *Ibid.,* p. 8.
[57] *Ibid.,* pp. 10–15.
[58] *Ibid.,* p. 17.

. . . stresses education for its own sake and as a means for the development of self-expression—orientations which the culturally deprived do not share. Furthermore, the discrimination unwittingly practiced in the school [against the culturally deprived child] aggravates the problems, and produces the schism between school and education.[59]

Some of the specific suggestions that Riessman offers are: that reading materials more suited to the culturally deprived be developed; that school know-how be developed in these children (how to ask and answer questions and how to study, for example); that new approaches involving more action be developed for teaching art, music, and social studies, subjects that Reissman believes are not interesting to the disadvantaged as they are currently taught; that the anti-intellectualism of the disadvantaged be combated, that they be helped to see the practical value of ideas and theories; and that the school be masculinized, (less emphasis should be placed upon the feminine values of conformity, dependence, neatness, and nonaggression, for instance).[60]

There are many educational programs for the disadvantaged now provided by the federal government. For example, the U.S. Office of Education lists in its publication *Programs for the Disadvantaged* the following types of program activities: research, personnel training, preschool education, elementary and secondary education, adult education, vocational education, student financial aid, construction, resources and equipment, supplementary educational activities, related educational services, and technical services.[61] Many of these program activities come under the National Defense Education Act of 1958, the Economic Opportunities Act of 1964, and the Elementary and Secondary Education Act of 1965 discussed in Chapter 6. Others result from legislation like the Civil Rights Act of 1964, the Vocational Education Act of 1963, and the Higher Education Act of 1965. Probably the best known program has been the Head Start program referred to in

[59] Frank Riessman, *op. cit.*, p. 15.
[60] *Ibid.*, pp. 30–35.
[61] U.S. Department of Health, Education, and Welfare, Office of Education, *Programs for the Disadvantaged*, (Washington, D.C.: U.S. Government Printing Office, 1966), p. 5.

Chapter 2. Head Start attempts to reduce educational deficiencies of disadvantaged children through preschool experiences. Though Head Start has been generally successful, it is not the quick-and-easy solution that some have believed it to be. The gains of the program can be quickly lost if there is not an effective follow up by good teachers and a suitable school program.

While all of the federal programs have been helpful, they have by no means solved the problems of the disadvantaged. It must be admitted that when one views the immensity and complexity of these problems one wonders how and when they will ever be solved. Surely the ultimate solution goes beyond what the school can do, for the problems are very much civic problems.[62] Whatever the school does, the child still goes back each day to the same disadvantaged environment. The problems of broken homes, neglectful parents, poor housing, lack of jobs, and discrimination still are there. Unless and until some real progress is made in these areas, it is doubtful that the school's efforts will make a significant difference for the majority of the disadvantaged. In the meantime, however, the school must do all that it can for its socially and culturally deprived students. Their disadvantages must be viewed as ". . . deriving from the circumstances of their past or present lives. It is the business of the school and of the whole society to strive to overcome these disadvantages."[63]

SUGGESTED ACTIVITIES

1. Investigate and prepare a report on the provisions made by your state for the education of exceptional children.
2. Interview a teacher of mentally retarded children about the nature of her work. Prepare a report for class presentation.
3. Arrange with your instructor to visit a school serving disadvantaged children. Prepare a written summary of your reactions to the visit.
4. Select a committee to prepare and present a debate to the class on the pros and cons of ability grouping.

[62] Fred M. Hechinger, "Rescue Operation for the Urban School," *New York Times*, July 16, 1967, sec. 4, p. 16.
[63] Educational Policies Commission, *op. cit.*, p. 18.

5. With your instructor's approval, invite an administrator whose school offers special programs for the gifted to speak to the class about these programs.
6. Consult the professional literature and government publications on education for the disadvantaged and prepare a report on a particular program currently being provided for such students by the federal government.
7. Compile a list of ten things that you will do as a teacher to provide for the slow learners in your classes. Be sure to make use of authoritative sources in compiling your list.

SELECTED REFERENCES

American Educational Research Association. "Education for Socially Disadvantaged Children," *Review of Educational Research,* Vol. 35, No. 6, December, 1965. Reviews research on such topics as the characteristics of socially disadvantaged children, their language development, learning disabilities, and programs and practices in compensatory education.

American Educational Research Association. "Education of Exceptional Children," *Review of Educational Research,* Vol. 36, No. 1, February, 1966. Reviews research for the previous three years on exceptional children, preparation of special education personnel, and organization, administration, and supervision of special education.

Conant, James B. *Slums and Suburbs.* New York: McGraw-Hill Book Company, 1961. A study of schools and student needs in metropolitan areas. Discusses schools in city slums and wealthy suburbs.

Cruickshank, William M., and Johnson, G. Orville, eds. *Education of Exceptional Children and Youth.* Second edition. Englewood Cliffs, N.J.: Prentice-Hall, 1967. A survey of the field with chapters on the various areas of exceptionality.

DeHaan, Robert F. *Accelerated Learning Programs.* The Library of Education. Washington, D.C.: The Center for Applied Research in Education, 1963. An overview of programs for gifted students. Enrichment, acceleration, and grouping are discussed along with the curriculum, the learning process, and the role of the teacher in such programs.

DeHaan, Robert F., and Havighurst, Robert J. *Educating Gifted Children* Revised edition. Chicago: The University of Chicago Press,

1961. An excellent statement of experience and research about the academically talented.

Educational Policies Commission. *American Education and the Search for Equal Opportunity.* Washington, D.C.: National Educational Association, 1965. A brief statement of the problem of providing equal opportunity and the role of the school in overcoming the problem. Some good recommendations are given for the special problem of *de facto* segregation.

Educational Policies Commission. *Education and the Disadvantaged American.* Washington, D.C.: National Education Association, 1962. Discusses the great problem of the schools in attempting to aid culturally deprived children to become all that they are capable of becoming.

Hildreth, Gertrude H. *Introduction to the Gifted.* New York: McGraw-Hill Book Company, 1966. Describes the gifted and the provisions education can make for this type of student. Chapters on the gifted in the elementary and in the secondary school.

Gallagher, James J. *Teaching the Gifted Child.* Boston: Allyn and Bacon, 1964. Within a broad concept of giftedness, the author presents information on the gifted with attention centered on instructional processes.

Johnson, G. Orville. *Education for the Slow Learners.* Englewood Cliffs, N.J.: Prentice-Hall, 1963. A work on the total problem of the slow learner and how the school can provide for him.

Loretan, Joseph O., and Umans, Shelley. *Teaching the Disadvantaged.* New York: Teachers College Press, Columbia University, 1966. Discusses new curriculum approaches and questions many notions about how to educate the disadvantaged.

National Education Association, Project on Instruction. *Schools for the Sixties.* New York: McGraw-Hill Book Company, 1963. Deals in depth with the crucial problems of good education for today's students.

Passow, A. Harry, Goldberg, Miriam, and Tannenbaum, Abraham, eds. *Education of the Disadvantaged: A Book of Readings.* New York: Holt, Rinehart and Winston, 1967. A collection of readings dealing with theoretical and practical aspects of the problem of providing education for the disadvantaged.

Riessman, Frank. *The Culturally Deprived Child.* New York: Harper & Row, Publishers, 1962. A small but valuable book. See particularly

Chapter IV, "The Culture of the Underprivileged: A New Look."
Strom, Robert D. *Teaching in the Slum School*. Columbus, Ohio: Charles E. Merrill Books, 1965. An overview of important concerns in the teaching of inner-city children. See especially Chapter 5, "Classroom Instruction."
Terman, Lewis M., ed. *Genetic Studies of Genius*. Five volumes. Stanford, California: Stanford University Press, 1925, 1926, 1930, 1947, 1959. A classic study of the gifted child.
U.S. Department of Health, Education, and Welfare, Office of Education. *Equality of Educational Opportunity*. Washington, D.C.: U.S. Government Printing Office, 1966. A summary of the larger report of a survey required under the Civil Rights Act of 1964 to determine the status of equal educational opportunity.

Appendix A: Professional Periodicals

The following list is intended to be illustrative of the wide range of professional periodicals available:

The American Biology Teacher. National Association of Biology Teachers, Jordan Hall, Indiana University, Bloomington, Ind. 47401. $8. (9 issues, Oct.–May)

American Educational Research Journal. American Educational Research Association, NEA, 1201 Sixteenth Street, N.W., Washington, D.C. 20036. $6. (4 times per year)

The American Historical Review. Macmillan Co. for The American Historical Association, 866 Third Avenue, New York, N.Y. 10022. $10. (quarterly in Oct., Jan., Apr., and July)

The American Journal of Sociology. University of Chicago Press, 5750 Ellis Avenue, Chicago, Ill. 60637. $6. (bimonthly)

The American Music Teacher. 2209 Carew Tower, Cincinnati, Ohio 45202. $3. (bimonthly)

American Sociological Review. American Sociological Association, 1755 Masschusetts Avenue, N.W., Washington, D.C. 20036. $10. (bimonthly)

American Vocational Journal. American Vocational Association, 1025 Fifteenth Street, N.W., Washington, D.C. 20005. $3. (monthly, Sept.–May)

The Arithmetic Teacher. National Council of Teachers of Mathematics, NEA, 1201 Sixteenth Street, N.W., Washington, D.C. 20036. $5. (monthly, Oct.–May)

Art Education. National Art Education Association, NEA, 1201 Sixteenth Street, N.W., Washington, D.C. 20036. $3. (monthly, Oct.–June)

Audiovisual Instruction. Department of Audiovisual Instruction, NEA, 1201 Sixteenth Street, N.W., Washington, D.C. 20036. $5. (monthly, except July and Aug.)

The Bulletin of the National Association of Secondary-School Principals, National Association of Secondary-School Principals, NEA, 1201 Sixteenth Street, N.W., Washington, D.C. 20036. $15. (monthly, 9 times a year)

Business Education Forum. National Business Education Association, NEA, 1201 Sixteenth Street, N.W., Washington, D.C. 20036. $5. (monthly, Oct.–May)

Childhood Education. Association for Childhood Education International, 3615 Wisconsin Avenue, N.W., Washington, D.C. 20016. $5.50. (monthly, Sept.–May)

The Clearing House. Fairleigh Dickinson University, Teaneck, N.J. 07666. $4.50. (monthly, Sept.–May)

Current History. 1822 Ludlow Street, Philadelphia, Pa. 19103. $8. (monthly)

Education Digest. Prakken Publications, 416 Longshore Drive, Ann Arbor, Mich. 48107. $5. (monthly, Sept.–May)

Elementary English. National Council of Teachers of English, 508 South Sixth Street, Champaign, Ill. 61822. $5. (monthly, Oct.–May)

Elementary School Journal. University of Chicago, 5835 Kimbark Avenue, Chicago, Ill. 60637. $4.50. (8 times a year)

English Journal. National Council of Teachers of English, 508 South Sixth Street, Champaign, Ill. 61822. $5. (monthly, Sept.–May)

Exceptional Children. Council for Exceptional Children, NEA, 1201 Sixteenth Street, N.W., Washington, D.C. 20036. $7. (9 issues per year, Sept.–May)

Grade Teacher. Educational Publishing Corp., Darien, Conn. 06820. $5.50. (monthly)

Harvard Educational Review. Graduate School of Education, Harvard University, Cambridge, Mass. 02138. $4. (quarterly)

The Horn Book. 585 Boylston Street, Boston, Mass. 02116. $5. (bimonthly)

Instructor. F. A. Owen Publishing Co., Dansville, N.Y. 14437. $6. (monthly)

Journal of Chemical Education. Division of Chemical Education, American Chemical Society, Easton, Pa. 18042. $4. (monthly)

Journal of Educational Psychology. American Psychological Association, 1200 Seventeenth Street, N.W., Washington, D.C. 20036. $8. (bimonthly)

The Journal of Educational Research. Dembar Educational Research Services, Box 1605, Madison, Wis. 53701. $7.50. (10 times a year)

Journal of Geography. A. J. Nystrom and Co., 3333 Elston Avenue, Chicago, Ill. 60618. $5. (monthly, except July and Aug.)

Journal of Health, Physical Education, and Recreation. American Association for Health, Physical Education, and Recreation, NEA, 1201 Sixteenth Street, N.W., Washington, D.C. 20036. $10. (9 issues a year)

Journal of Home Economics. American Home Economics Association, 1600 Twentieth Street, N.W., Washington, D.C. 20009. With AHEA membership of $20. (10 issues yearly)

The Journal of Industrial Arts Education. American Industrial Arts Association, NEA, 1201 Sixteenth Street, N.W., Washington, D.C. 20036. $6. (5 times during the school year)

Journal of Reading. International Reading Association, Box 119, Newark, Del. 19711. $4.50. (6 issues a year)

Journal of School Health. American School Health Association, 515 East Main Street, Kent, Ohio 44240. Membership $5; single copies $1. (10 issues a year)

Journal of Teacher Education. National Commission on Teacher Education and Professional Standards, NEA, 1201 Sixteenth Street, N.W., Washington, D.C. 20036. $3. (quarterly)

The Mathematics Teacher. National Council of Teachers of Mathematics, NEA, 1201 Sixteenth Street, N.W., Washington, D.C. 20036. $5. (monthly, Oct.–May)

Music Educators Journal. Music Educators National Conference, NEA, 1201 Sixteenth Street, N.W., Washington, D.C. 20036. $3.50. (bimonthly)

NEA Journal. National Education Association, 1201 Sixteenth Street, N.W., Washington, D.C. 20036. Free to members of the Association; single copies 80 cents. (monthly, Sept.–May)

The National Elementary Principal. Department of Elementary School Principals, NEA, 1201 Sixteenth Street, N.W., Washington, D.C. 20036. $5.50. (monthly for 6 months)

The Personnel and Guidance Journal. American Personnel and Guidance Association, 1605 New Hampshire Avenue, N.W., Washington, D.C. 20009. $10. (10 issues, Sept.–June)

Phi Delta Kappan. Phi Delta Kappa, Eighth Street and Union Avenue, Bloomington, Ind. 47401. $5. (monthly)

School Arts. Davis Press, Inc., Printers Building, Worcester, Mass. 01608. $7. (monthly, Sept.–June)

The School Counselor. American School Counselor Association, 1605 New Hampshire Avenue, N.W., Washington, D.C. 20009. $4. (quarterly)

School Review. Department of Education Publications, University of Chicago, Chicago, Ill. 60637. $5. (quarterly)

Science. American Association for the Advancement of Science, 1515 Massachusetts Avenue, N.W., Washington, D.C. 20005. $8.50. (weekly)

Science and Children. National Science Teachers Association, NEA, 1201 Sixteenth Street, N.W., Washington, D.C. 20036. $4. (8 issues a year)

The Science Teacher. National Science Teachers Association, NEA, 1201 Sixteenth Street, N.W., Washington, D.C. 20036. $10. (monthly)

Scientific American. 2 West 45th Street, New York, N.Y. 10017. $6. (monthly)

The Social Studies. McKinley Publishing Co., 112 South New Broadway, Brooklawn, N.J. 08030. $5. (monthly, Oct.–April)

The Speech Teacher. Speech Association of America, Statler Hilton Hotel, New York, N.Y. 10001. $10. (quarterly)

Teachers College Record. Teachers College, Columbia University, New York, N.Y. 10027. $5. (monthly, Oct.–May)

Appendix B: Suggested Films

The following 16 mm. sound films are suggested for use with this book. Information supplied includes the source from which each film is available.

"A Day in the Life of a Five Year Old." Metropolitan School Study Council, 525 West 120th Street, New York, N.Y., 19 minutes, black and white. Young children are pictured in a well-planned and well-equipped kindergarten. Also points out the role of the kindergarten teacher.

"And No Bells Ring." Sterling Movies, Inc., Chicago, Ill., 56 minutes, black and white. Reviews the "Trump Report" on the reorganization of the secondary school staff. Large-group and small-group instruction are part of the plan along with independent study and the use of teacher assistants.

"A University Is a Teacher." University of Southern California, Department of Cinema, Film Distribution Division, University Park, Los Angeles, Calif., 30 minutes, black and white. Outstanding professors at the University of Southern California are shown in classrooms and counseling students on research projects.

"Breakthrough in Education." National Education Association, 29½ minutes, black and white. A television discussion of some new developments in education such as teaching machines, instructional television, and curriculum changes.

"Challenge of the Gifted." McGraw-Hill, New York, N.Y., 12 minutes, color. Shows how the needs of gifted students in intermediate grades are met in the program of the Vallejo, California, United School District.

"Design of American Public Education." McGraw-Hill, New York, N.Y., 15 minutes, black and white. An animated presentation comparing a highly centralized kind of organization for education with a decentralized system which better fits needs of the local community and its students.

"The Dropout." Mental Health Film Board, Inc., 164 East 38th Street, New York, N.Y., 28 minutes, black and white. The story of a high school dropout—what contributed to the problem and ways in which it could be solved.

"Education in America." A three-film series: "The Seventeenth and Eighteenth Centuries," "The Nineteenth Century," and "The Twentieth Century." Coronet Films, New York, N.Y., 16 minutes each, color. Reviews highlights of the historical development of American education.

"High School Team Teaching: The Ferris Story." Bailey Films, Inc., 6509 DeLongpre Avenue, Hollywood, Calif., 26 minutes, color. Follows teachers and students through their daily schedules in a team teaching program at Ferris High School, Spokane, Washington.

"If These Were Your Children." Metropolitan Life Insurance Company, 1 Madison Avenue, New York, N.Y., Part I, 25 minutes, Part II, 21 minutes, color. Seven behavior types found in second grade are discussed by four experts.

"Mike Makes His Mark." National Education Association, 29 minutes, color. Views the junior high school in action. Stresses the role of guidance in dealing with problems of Mike, who wants to quit school.

"Not by Chance." National Education Association, 28 minutes, color. A teacher education program is viewed through the story of Donna, a college student preparing to teach secondary science. The importance of a good program is emphasized.

"Operation Head Start." Bailey Films, Inc., 6509 DeLongpre Avenue, Hollywood, Calif., 16 minutes, black and white. Shows what a Head Start child development center did for an underprivileged child.

"Portrait of the Inner City." McGraw-Hill, New York, N.Y., 17 minutes, black and white. Presents positive and negative aspects of life in the inner city and the people who influence Tommy Knight, a Negro boy.

"Portrait of the Inner City School: A Place to Learn." McGraw-Hill, New York, N.Y., 19 minutes, black and white. Illustrates various teaching techniques used with disadvantaged children and ways in which schools sometimes unknownly discriminate against such children.

"Rafe: Developing Giftedness in the Educationally Disadvantaged." Bailey Films, Inc., 6509 DeLongpre Avenue, Hollywood, Calif., 20 minutes, color. Portrays the ways in which teachers and counselors worked to bring out Rafe's potentialities.

"Section Sixteen." Westinghouse Broadcasting Company, 14 minutes, black and white. The historical development of free, compulsory education in the United States is described.

"Skippy and the Three R's." National Education Association, 29 minutes, color. Illustrates a good first-grade program through the experience of Skippy Gordon, who is just beginning school. Sound instructional practices are also presented.

"Teaching Machines and Programmed Learning." National Education Association, 29 minutes, black and white. Illustrates the use of programmed instruction and automated teaching devices as well as surveying techniques and principles involved.

"The Hickory Stick." International Film Bureau, 332 South Michigan Avenue, Chicago, Ill., 28 minutes, black and white. An approach to discipline that does not require "the hickory stick" to help students control their feelings and accept authority is presented.

"The Junior High School Story." National Association of Secondary School Principals of the National Education Association, 28 minutes, color. Selected California schools are used to illustrate varied junior high school programs, activities, and facilities.

"The Nature and Function of Higher Education." Pyramid Film Producers, Box 1048, Santa Monica, Calif., 18 minutes, black and white. Presents the college as a world waiting to be explored and the student as explorer.

"The Three R's Plus." Mental Health Film Board, Inc., 164 East 38th Street, New York, N.Y., 27 minutes, black and white or color. Portrays good educational techniques; considers both gifted and handicapped children.

"The Time of Their Lives." National Education Association, 29 minutes, black and white. A typical class in action demonstrates the value of kindergarten.

"Who Is Pete?" International Film Bureau, 332 South Michigan Avenue, Chicago, Ill., 27 minutes, black and white or color. Illustrates the use of tests to determine the ability, readiness, achievement, and aptitude of a sixth-grade student.

Appendix C: Code of Ethics of the Education Profession[1]

PREAMBLE

We, professional educators of the United States of America, affirm our belief in the worth and dignity of man. We recognize the supreme importance of the pursuit of truth, the encouragement of scholarship, and the promotion of democratic citizenship. We regard as essential to these goals the protection of freedom to learn and to teach and the guarantee of equal educational opportunity for all. We affirm and accept our responsibility to practice our profession according to the highest ethical standards.

We acknowledge the magnitude of the profession we have chosen, and engage ourselves, individually and collectively, to judge our colleagues and to be judged by them in accordance with the applicable provisions of this Code.

PRINCIPLE 1

Commitment to the Student

We measure success by the progress of each student toward achievement of his maximum potential. We therefore work to stimulate the spirit of inquiry, the acquisition of knowledge and understanding, and the thoughtful formulation of worthy goals. We recognize the im-

[1] Adopted by the Representative Assembly of the National Education Association, 1963

portance of cooperative relationships with other community institutions, especially the home.

In fulfilling our obligations to the student, we—
1. Deal justly and considerately with each student.
2. Encourage the student to study varying points of view and respect his right to form his own judgment.
3. Withhold confidential information about a student or his home unless we deem that its release serves professional purposes, benefits the student, or is required by law.
4. Make discreet use of available information about the student.
5. Conduct conferences with or concerning students in an appropriate place and manner.
6. Refrain from commenting unprofessionally about a student or his home.
7. Avoid exploiting our professional relationship with any student.
8. Tutor only in accordance with officially approved policies.
9. Inform appropriate individuals and agencies of the student's educational needs and assist in providing an understanding of his educational experiences.
10. Seek constantly to improve learning facilities and opportunities.

PRINCIPLE 2

Commitment to the Community

We believe that patriotism in its highest form requires dedication to the principles of our democratic heritage. We share with all other citizens the responsibility for the development of sound public policy. As educators, we are particularly accountable for participating in the development of educational programs and policies and for interpreting them to the public.

In fulfilling our obligations to the community, we—
1. Share the responsibility for improving the educational opportunities for all.
2. Recognize that each educational institution may have a person authorized to interpret its official policies.
3. Acknowledge the right and responsibility of the public to participate in the formulation of educational policy.

4. Evaluate through appropriate professional procedures conditions within a district or institution of learning, make known serious deficiencies, and take any action deemed necessary and proper.
5. Use educational facilities for intended purposes consistent with applicable policy, law, and regulation.
6. Assume full political and citizenship responsibilities, but refrain from exploiting the institutional privileges of our professional positions to promote political candidates or partisan activities.
7. Protect the educational program against undesirable infringement.

PRINCIPLE 3

Commitment to the Profession

We believe that the quality of the services of the education profession directly influences the future of the nation and its citizens. We therefore exert every effort to raise educational standards, to improve our service, to promote a climate in which the exercise of professional judgment is encouraged, and to achieve conditions which attract persons worthy of the trust to careers in education. Aware of the value of united effort, we contribute actively to the support, planning, and programs of our professional organizations.

In fulfilling our obligations to the profession, we—

1. Recognize that a profession must accept responsibility for the conduct of its members and understand that our own conduct may be regarded as representative.
2. Participate and conduct ourselves in a responsible manner in the development and implementation of policies affecting education.
3. Cooperate in the selective recruitment of prospective teachers and in the orientation of student teachers, interns, and those colleagues new to their positions.
4. Accord just and equitable treatment to all members of the profession in the exercise of their professional rights and responsibilities, and support them when unjustly accused or mistreated.
5. Refrain from assigning professional duties to nonprofessional personnel when such assignment is not in the best interest of the student.
6. Provide, upon request, a statement of specific reason for administrative recommendations that lead to the denial of increments, significant changes in employment, or termination of employment.

7. Refrain from exerting undue influence based on the authority of our positions in the determination of professional decisions by colleagues.

8. Keep the trust under which confidential information is exchanged.

9. Make appropriate use of time granted for professional purposes.

10. Interpret and use the writings of others and the findings of educational research with intellectual honesty.

11. Maintain our integrity when dissenting by basing our public criticism of education on valid assumptions as established by careful evaluation of facts or hypotheses.

12. Represent honestly our professional qualifications and identify ourselves only with reputable educational institutions.

13. Respond accurately to requests for evaluations of colleagues seeking professional positions.

14. Provide applicants seeking information about a position with an honest description of the assignment, the conditions of work, and related matters.

PRINCIPLE 4

Commitment to Professional Employment Practices

We regard the employment agreement as a solemn pledge to be executed both in spirit and in fact in a manner consistent with the highest ideals of professional service. Sound professional personnel relationships with governing boards are built upon personal integrity, dignity, and mutual respect.

In fulfilling our obligations to professional employment practices, we—

1. Apply for or offer a position on the basis of professional and legal qualifications.

2. Apply for a specific position only when it is known to be vacant and refrain from such practices as underbidding or commenting adversely about other candidates.

3. Fill no vacancy except where the terms, conditions, policies, and practices permit the exercise of our professional judgment and skill, and where a climate conducive to professional service exists.

4. Adhere to the conditions of a contract or to the terms of an appointment until either has been terminated legally or by mutual consent.

5. Give prompt notice of any change in availability of service, in status of applications, or in change in position.
6. Conduct professional business through the recognized educational and professional channels.
7. Accept no gratuities or gifts of significance that might influence our judgment in the exercise of our professional duties.
8. Engage in no outside employment that will impair the effectiveness of our professional service and permit no commercial exploitation of our professional position.

Index

221